CONTENTS

CD TRACKS

TRACK	DESCRIPTION
1	Figure 1.4 Progression 1 Play Along
2	Figure 1.6 Solo Demonstration
3	Figure 1.9 Progression 2 Play Along
4	Figure 1.10 Progression 3 Play Along
5	Figure 2.3 Progression Play Along Tempo 1
6	Figure 2.3 Progression Play Along Tempo 2
7	Figure 2.3 Practice Demonstration
8	Figure 2.4 Solo Demonstration
9	Figure 2.5 Play Along
10	Figure 2.6 Play Along
11	Figure 3.5 Demonstration
12	Figure 3.5 Play Along
13	Figure 3.6 C Minor Play Along
14	Figure 3.6 G Minor Play Along
15	Figure 3.7 C Minor Play Along
16	Figure 3.7 E Minor Play Along
17	Figure 3.8 Play Along
18	Figure 3.9 Play Along
19	Figure 3.10 Play Along
20	Figure 3.11 Play Along
21	Figure 4.4 Play Along
22	Figure 4.3 Phrases with 4.4 Play Along
23	Figure 4.4 Demonstrating Blues Scale Practice
24	Figure 4.10 Play Along
25	Figure 4.11 Play Along
26	Figure 5.4 Approach Note Demonstration
27	Figure 5.5 Solo Demonstration
28	Figure 5.11 Play Along
29	Figure 5.8 Line Demonstrated with 5.11 Play Along
30	Figure 5.12 Play Along
31	Figure 5.16 Play Along
32	Figure 5.17 Play Along
33	Figure 5.13 Line Demonstrated with 5.16 Play Along
34	Figure 5.19 Bebop Demonstration
35	Figure 6.7 Play Along
36	Figure 6.23 Play Along
37	Figure 6.24 Play Along
38	Figure 7.2 Play Along
39	Figure 7.2 Solo Demonstration
40	Figure 7.4 Play Along

INTRODUCTION

Improvisation is the art of real-time composition. Having a large musical vocabulary enables you to create memorable solos that express your feelings during each performance. This book will guide you through exploring some of the many possible scale choices that can be used with chords and chord progressions, giving you a greater range of expression.

To get the most out of the lessons in this book, you should have the ability to play major and minor scales and understand basic harmony. Please refer to my first book *Piano Essentials: Scales, Chords, Arpeggios, and Cadences for the Contemporary Pianist* (Berklee Press, 2005) as a source for review.

There is the well-known philosophical dilemma that asks, "Which came first, the chicken or the egg?" Perhaps a similar musical question might be "Which came first, the scale or the chord?"

In truth, each exists as part of the other. While it is possible to determine the notes for a scale based on a given chord, it is equally possible to come up with chords based on a scale. Over the centuries, musicians have established a system of sonic descriptions and analysis. Let's examine how to apply the results to our own improvisations.

We will start with a quick review of some theory. (Please make sure these concepts are clear to you, or you will have great difficulty properly applying the scales.)

CHAPTER 1

Basics of Chord-Scale Improvisation

A *scale* is a series of pitches arranged in either ascending or descending order. There are many possibilities, but the major scale is one of the most common and will be used as a starting point to further explore musical relationships.

A *major scale* can be formed from any starting pitch using a series of whole steps and half steps, such as the C major scale shown in figure 1.1.

Fig. 1.1. The C Major Scale

We can create triads or seventh chords from this scale by building upwards diatonically in intervals of thirds.

TIP: BUILDING CHORDS FROM THIRDS AND FOURTHS

Using thirds to create chords (*tertian* harmony) is the traditional method, but not the only one. For example, using fourths (*quartal* harmony) is commonplace in jazz and other contemporary styles.

Starting from each note of any major scale, we can create seven possible triads or seventh chords. The resulting chords are *diatonic* chords—chords built entirely of notes within the scale.

Chord Construction Based on Scale: **Position:**

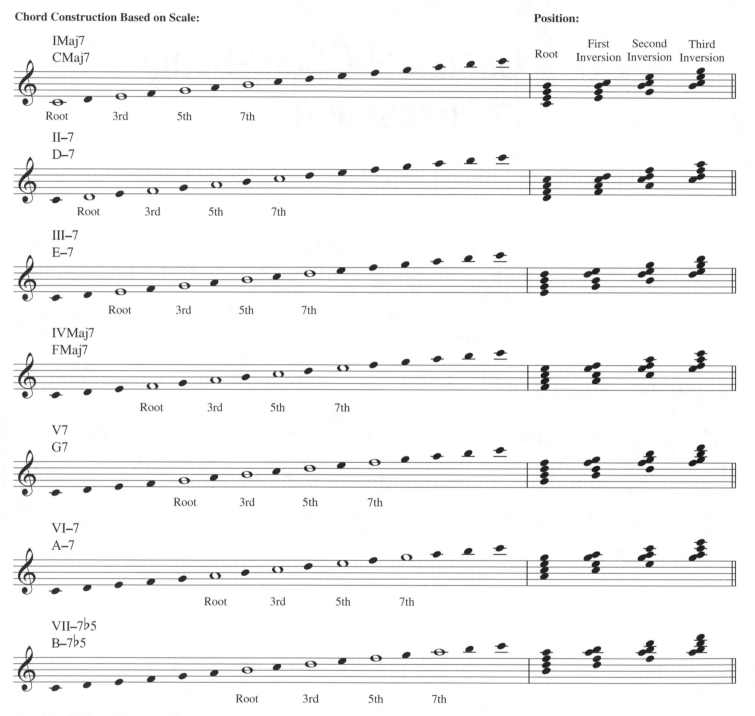

Fig. 1.2. C Major Diatonic Chords

We label chords based on their relationship to the first note of the scale using Roman numerals. Figure 1.3 shows all major-key diatonic seventh chords in root position and their corresponding Roman numerals.

Fig. 1.3. Diatonic Seventh Chords in All Major Keys

Notice that the Roman numerals labeling the chords are the same for each key. All major keys share the same harmonic relationships between diatonic chords. That is to say, using any major key signature, all I chords are major, all II chords are minor, all III chords are minor, etc.

Understanding these relationships helps determine the appropriate scales to use while improvising and facilitates the ability to play songs in any key.

Be sure that you are comfortable playing major scales, arpeggios, and diatonic chords. Mastering these building blocks is an important step in developing your ability to improvise.

Look at the chord progression in figure 1.4. By examining its chords, we can see that the progression is built entirely from chords occurring in the key of G. Since this progression uses only diatonic chords, it's safe to assume notes from the G major scale will sound good being used to create an improvised melody.

TRACK 1

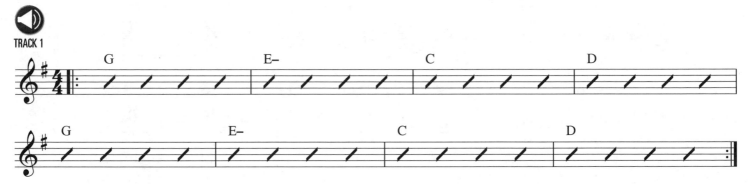

Fig. 1.4. Progression 1

If you have never improvised, being asked to do so may seem like an impossible task. An important point to remember is that learning to improvise includes making a lot of mistakes. In classical training, mistakes are considered unacceptable, but in order to improvise, you will need to remove the worry of hitting a wrong note!

If you are improvising, there are no wrong notes; you are writing the score as you play. You might accidentally hit notes that don't sound the way you want, but playing these notes is an important part of the experience.

While listening to play-along track 1, improvise a simple melody over progression 1 using only notes from a G major scale.

IMPROVISATION TIP

Improvisation isn't just a matter of choosing notes; it includes the choice of rhythm, dynamics, and phrasing (and when to rest!). For now, keep it simple, and listen to how each note in the scale sounds against the given chord progression. We'll work on many exercises to develop your ideas later.

What did you notice about the sound of the major scale as you improvised over the progression?

Here are a few specific things to listen for:

- Playing a chord tone will sound strong and resolved. For instance, as the music moves through the progression, playing the root, 3rd, or 5th of each chord will sound very harmonious.

- When playing the I major chord, the note that is a 4th above the root sounds dissonant. In many music theory books, the 4th note above a major chord is labeled an "avoid" note. All musical note relationships are useful, so rather than avoid it all together, listen carefully and learn to recognize how it sounds so you can use it by choice when creating a musical phrase.

Fig. 1.5. Sounds Dissonant against C Major (4th over I)

In summary, all notes can be used. Some notes provide a sense of resolution, while others provide a sense of tension and seem to want to move toward a resolution.

Using the same diatonic progression, figure 1.6 is an example of an improvised melody using primarily chord tones. The other scalar notes are used to connect from one chord tone to the next. (These other notes are often referred to as *passing tones*.) All of the notes are diatonic to the key signature.

Listen to the melody in figure 1.6, based on progression 1.

Fig. 1.6. Melodic on Progression 1 with Analysis

Here are two new progressions. Try to analyze the chords and determine what keys they are in. They are both completely diatonic to one major key. If you remember that chords diatonic to a single major key only have a single dominant chord (the V7), the analysis will be easy. If a diatonic progression is only using triads, then it becomes slightly more difficult, but looking at the distances between the major and minor chords will still lead you to a single solution.

Fig. 1.7. Progression 2

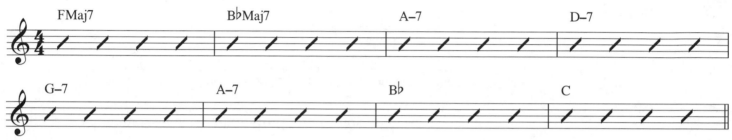

Fig. 1.8. Progression 3

Turn the book upside-down to see the analysis and key signature for each progression. Check them after you have tried to analyze them on your own.

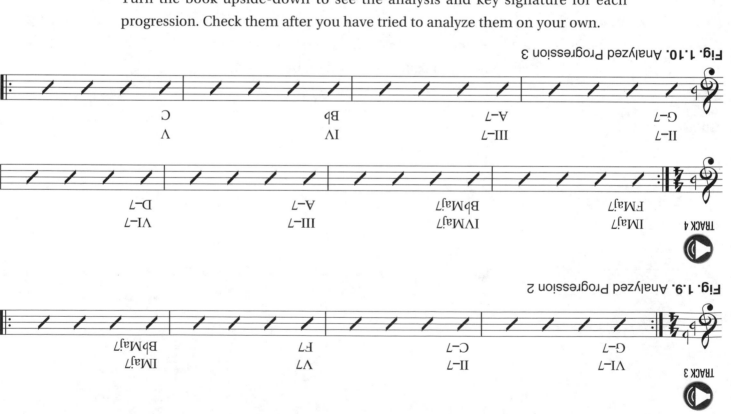

Fig. 1.10. Analyzed Progression 3

Fig. 1.9. Analyzed Progression 2

Use the play-along tracks to practice improvising diatonically over the progressions. Listen carefully as you play notes that are consonant and dissonant in relation to the chords. Remember that the experience of playing both "good" and "bad" sounding notes is important as you learn the sounds of each musical relationship.

It is important that you practice slow enough that your ears can hear what you are playing, and your mind can comprehend what you are doing. You may want to start practicing without the play along until you feel comfortable with the progressions. One of the keys to a musician's development is having the patience to practice slowly and accurately.

For now, don't be overly judgmental of the result of your improvisation. It takes a lot of practice and experience to feel comfortable with the language we are learning. When you listen to a great improviser's performance, they have played solos on similar chord progressions hundreds, if not thousands, of times. No musician has ever improvised at a professional level without years of practicing that particular skill.

IMPOSING LIMITS

To develop more command of the language, it's often helpful to limit your improvisation by imposing boundaries on your playing. These limitations cause you to focus on a single aspect rather than be overwhelmed with all of the possibilities inherent in improvising. Always practice the progression or songs you are working on with specific exercises first, and then without any boundaries.

The following exercise focuses on the root, 3rd, and 5th. It is common to create phrases that resolve to chord tones, so practicing these notes is a great way to begin.

EXERCISE 1.1. BASIC CHORD TONES

Practice improvising using chord tones with progression 1, 2, and 3, or using any progression you are working on. Follow the procedure shown.

1. Roots with whole notes.

Fig. 1.11. Roots with Whole Notes

2. Roots with improvised rhythm.
3. Repeat steps 1 and 2 using only the 3rds of each chord.
4. Repeat steps 1 and 2 using only the 5ths of each chord.
5. Practice steps 1 and 2 using any combination of root, 3rd, or 5th.

Fig. 1.12. Improvising Chord Tones and Rhythms

CHORD TONES AND TENSIONS

In reviewing the construction of diatonic chords, we stacked diatonic thirds starting from each note in a given major scale. We determined that these chord tones were the most consonant sounding notes to play on each chord in a diatonic progression (particularly the root, 3rd, and 5th). What if we keep going upwards?

There are only seven notes in a major scale, so we'll have to extend the scale example to two octaves in order to realize the possibilities. Look at the result starting on the root of our I major 7 chord in the key of C.

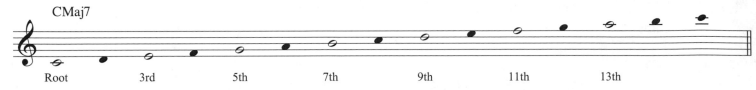

Fig. 1.13. CMaj7 with 9, 11, and 13

The result gives us intervals beyond the chord tone of the 7th and include the 9th, 11th, and 13th. These additional notes added to chords are called *tensions*, and provide us with sonic flavor.

The tensions indicated in figure 1.13 are the ones that naturally occur using the diatonic harmony of a major scale. If we extend the harmony outside of the diatonic realm of the major scale, the tensions can be changed (altered). The possibilities for a major triad and minor triad are listed in figure 1.14.

Fig. 1.14. C Root and Every Possible Intervallic Tension and Chord Tone

Tensions create more dissonance than chord tones, so their naming is quite appropriate. While at first you may feel some of these notes sound "weird" or just plain wrong, give them a chance. Like a good book or movie, we need some tension in our lives to go along with the consonance of perfect harmony.

Notice that while we label the tensions as 9, 11, and 13, it might be easier to recognize them as the 2nd, 4th, and 6th notes of a scale. When labeling chords, there are some differences, so writing C6 is not interpreted the same as writing C13, even though the 6th scale degree is the same note as the 13th.

When you encounter C9 or C13, it is implying that the chord is actually a C7 with the addition of the 9th or 13th. (In order to get to the 9th or 13th, you have to go past the 7th, so the 7th is implied.)

As you read through music lead sheets, you will notice that there are a number of different ways authors and publishers have chosen to label chords. Figure 1.15 is a chart showing the various chord qualities in root position. The first label, in bold, is the preferred choice at Berklee College of Music.

C major	**C**	C Maj	CM
C minor	**C–**	C min	Cm
C augmented	**C+**	C Aug	
C diminished	**C°**	C Dim	
C major 7	**CMaj7**	CM7, CΔ7	
C dominant 7	**C7**		
C minor 7	**C–7**	C min7	Cm7
C minor 7♭5	**C–7♭5**	Cø	
C diminished 7	**C°7**	Cdim7	

Fig. 1.15. Chord Symbols

To avoid confusion, the best way to label tensions is by using parenthesis after the chord label. For example:

C dominant 7 with tension ♭9 would be C7(♭9).

C major 7 with tension ♯11 would be CMaj7(♯11).

C major triad with tension 9 would be C(9).

To label a chord to be played over a specific bass note, use a back slash / . For example, a D♭ chord played over a C bass note would be D♭/C.

To label a chord over a chord (polychord or upper structure), use an underline. For example an A triad over a C7 would be: $\dfrac{\text{A}}{\text{C7}}$

In most cases, experienced players do not need anything more on a lead sheet than a chord symbol, because they will interpret tensions and voicings according to their own tastes. If you are looking for something that needs to be specific, then providing the appropriate tensions or upper structure in the label makes sense.

As we work with chord progressions in various styles, the application of tensions to the chords is often quite important in creating the sound of the harmony.

There are some differing opinions on what tensions are acceptable on what chords, and their acceptability greatly depends on the context of their function within the given chord progression. Figure 1.14 is a general guideline to the acceptable use of tensions. As we move forward in learning to improvise, you may want to reference this chart and try to include some of these tensions in your chord voicings.

I have included style-appropriate chord voicings with many of the musical examples.

Not all styles of music use all types of tensions. If you are trying to learn a specific style of music, start by emulating the harmonic, rhythmic, and melodic foundation it is created from before adventuring into new ground!

It can be quite overwhelming to think about all of the musical possibilities we have just described. In the next chapter, we will start by returning to the major scale and its diatonic harmony.

CHAPTER 2

Modes and How to Use Them

A *mode* is a form of something. In music, we use the word "mode" to describe various forms of a single scale. The first chapter reviewed the major scale and its diatonic chords. We built chords starting from each note of the major scale and used Roman numerals to label the result. Instead of chords, what happens if we build a new scale starting from each note of the major scale?

The resulting scales are modes of the major scale, as shown in figure 2.1.

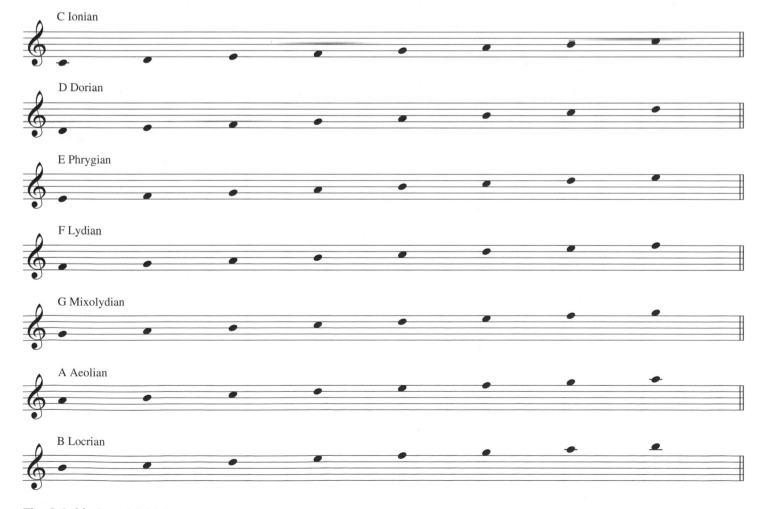

Fig. 2.1. Modes of C Major

USING MODES IN IMPROVISATION

Each mode shown in figure 2.1 is directly related to a diatonic chord, and understanding these relationships allows us to analyze a progression and practice playing scales and patterns that correctly fit the harmony. The progression shown in figure 2.2 could be analyzed as II–7 V7 IMaj7 in the key of C, which would mean D Dorian, G Mixolydian, and C Ionian chord scales would be commonly used.

Fig. 2.2. Progression with Modes

As we continue to work with songs, we'll see that many contain progressions that move through multiple key signatures, and studying these modes will make us ready to respond to the resulting harmonic shifts. There are often many scale choices that can be used with chords. (Remember all of those tension possibilities!) We want them all at our fingertips so that we can have the greatest freedom of expression.

When playing songs that have very few chord changes, it is also possible to impose modal changes in our improvisations that drastically shift the mood of our solo. For instance, playing a solo over E minor could start with Dorian mode, or Aeolian mode, and shift to Phrygian. Those are just some of the modes from a major scale; there are many others. We will experiment with these a little later.

Let's apply the modes to a song. Figure 2.3 is a common progression with its analysis. Since the chords are all diatonic to the key of F, we can easily apply our major scale modes to the progression.

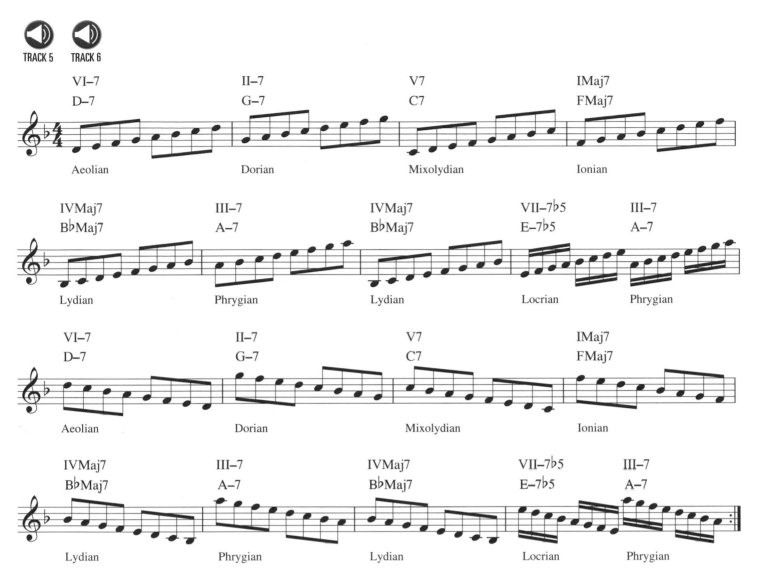

TRACK 5   TRACK 6

Fig. 2.3. Progression/Song Form

PRACTICE

TRACK 7

1. Play each chord scale from root to root ascending.
2. Play each chord scale from root to root descending.
3. Review exercises 1.1 on the above progression.
4. Freely combine the exercises into your own improvisation.

Progression through Four Major Keys 2

TRACK 10

Fig. 2.6. Progression through Four Major Keys 2

PARALLEL MODES

Because most musicians are very familiar with the major scale, let's look at the differences between a major scale and each major scale mode. For instance, C Dorian is the same as C major with a flat 3 and 7. The chart below illustrates the changes that occur in comparing the major scale with each mode we have learned so far.

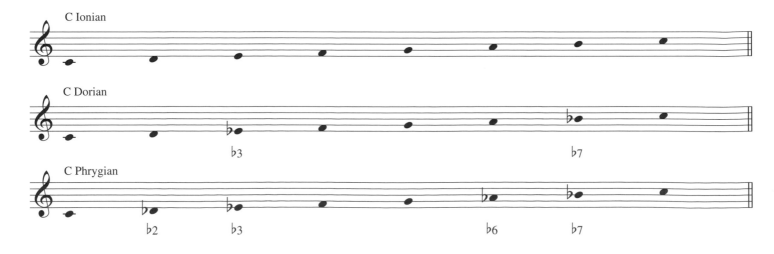

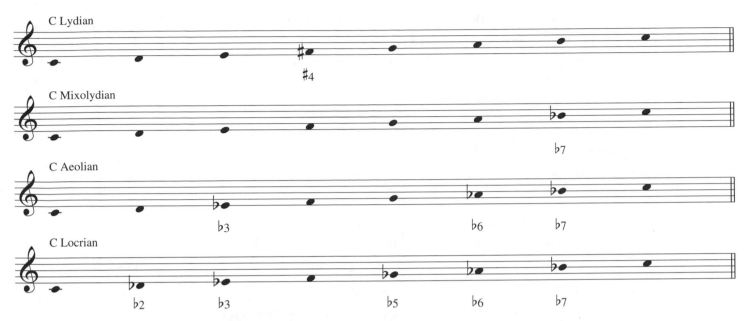

Fig. 2.7. C Major Scale Compared to Each Major Scale Mode

Eventually, you will not have to think at all in order to utilize these chord scales, but until then, having a few points of reference can be helpful in fully understanding them.

EXERCISE 2.2. BREATH AND PHRASING

Unlike singers and wind instrument players, keyboardists do not rely on their breath to create sound, and if we are not paying attention, it's easy to keep playing and not create any phrasing at all in our solos. Beyond the notes, a musical phrase is created by a number of factors such as: when it starts (upbeat, downbeat, middle of the measure, etc.), rhythmic construction, accents, dynamic shape (does it get louder or softer), and when it ends.

Let's try to get a sense of what musical ideas you have while playing the piano, and then without worrying about the piano or specific notes. You will need some sort of recording device for this exercise.

1. Record at least eight measures of you playing a piano solo with play-along track 4.

2. Record at least eight measures of you scat singing (or humming) a solo with play-along track 4. Don't worry about singing in tune or singing correct notes. The important part is to vocalize your ideas! Rather than be concerned with notes, think about the shape, moving up, down, repeating some notes, using interesting rhythms.

3. Transcribe your piano solo.

4. Transcribe your singing solo only with rhythms. (Try to include any obvious phrase marks, accents, and dynamics on both solos.)

5. Compare the phrasing.

In many cases, the singing solo has better phrasing and more interesting rhythms. There are two reasons for this. First, removing the worry of playing the right note creates a sense of freedom to improvise more adventurously. It is also much easier to only consider a single thing (rhythms) than multiple things (rhythms + notes). Second, when you sing, you need to stop to breathe. This naturally creates phrasing, which may or may not be currently integrated into your piano playing.

Compare and analyze what you liked or disliked about both solos. Where do the phrases start? If you always come in on the downbeat of a measure, then you need to work on creating phrases that start on the upbeats. If you always use eighth notes, then try to incorporate dotted rhythms, sixteenth notes, etc., into your playing.

If you like the rhythms of your scat solo, rewrite it with notes. You might have some pitches sung already, or a musical shape. Turn the shape into a solo using the chord scales we have studied. Try to get your phrases to resolve, so aim for ending them on a chord tone.

This exercise will help you find your voice as an improviser. Of course, we want to always be developing that voice to have more and more vocabulary. As you learn about modes and chords, this kind of exercise will help you use them to improvise solos with greater expression.

As we progress through the book, there will be various exercises designed to help you gain familiarity with navigating through chord changes and creating improvised melodies. Each exercise can be applied to any of the lessons, so be sure to go back and apply earlier exercises on the new material.

PRACTICE TIPS

Almost all music can be broken down into a relatively simple set of progressions. What makes some music more challenging is the movement in and out of different keys and modes, sometimes at rapid tempos. As you practice any skill, memorizing it in all keys will give you the ability to tackle these difficult songs more easily. I have included as many play-along examples as would fit on a CD, and suggest you continue your studies by looking at the various commercially available play-along books in the styles of greatest interest to you. As an alternative, creating your own audio or MIDI play-along tracks will be beneficial in developing these skills with a strong sense of time. Knowledge of the scales is not enough to make you an articulate improviser; you need to master them at any tempo so they can be used in creating dynamic solos that also include interesting rhythms and phrases.

I have included fingering charts for the most commonly used modes in the appendices.

- Start slowly to ensure accurate fingering, using separate hands if needed.
- Focus on one scale at a time through all keys.
- Keep track of your progress by using a practice journal.

- Keep a music manuscript book with you and write down additional examples for practice. This could include specific exercises you create, transcriptions of solos you have learned, or any musical idea you need to keep track of. I will reference your notebook in future chapters suggesting that you write out additional musical examples.

PRACTICE

Practice the modes in appendix. A, carefully adhering to the correct fingerings. Consistent mistake-free practice leads to a confident command of the language. Listen carefully to the sound of each scale as you play it. Knowing the sound of each mode allows you to readily use it in your improvisation.

Modes of Minor Scales

PURE NATURAL MINOR

The pure natural minor scale is identical to the Aeolian mode (chapter 2). It's built on the 6th scale degree of the major scale, and is also known as the *relative minor scale*. Any major scale and its relative minor scale share the same key signature.

Notice that the resulting modes of pure natural minor and major are the same, since the notes of the scales are identical (just occurring in a different order).

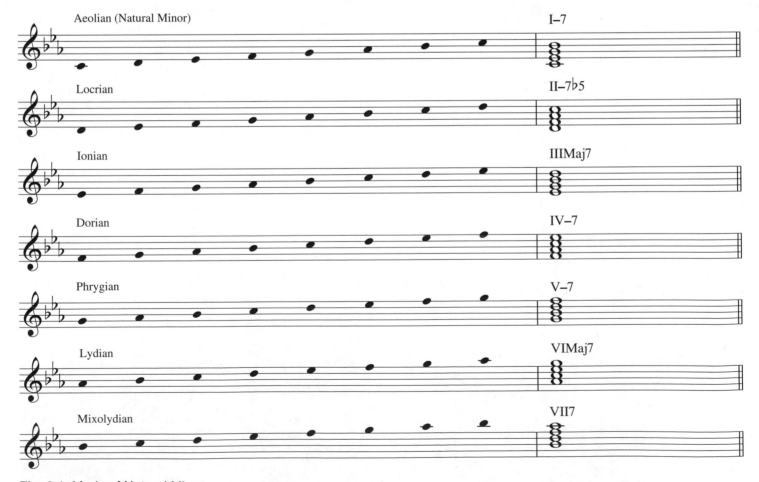

Fig. 3.1. Mode of Natural Minor

There are a number of scales based on alterations of pure natural minor that increase our musical options.

HARMONIC MINOR

The harmonic minor scale is created by raising the 7th scale degree of the pure natural minor scale half a step. The most significant change is the V7 chord quality, which is transformed from a minor 7 in pure natural minor to a dominant 7, resulting in a stronger resolution to the tonic. The chart below shows the corresponding harmony and modes resulting from the scale.

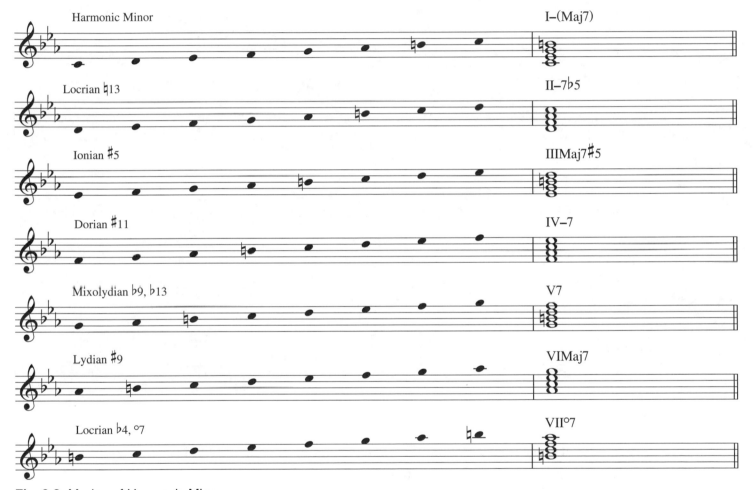

Fig. 3.2. Modes of Harmonic Minor

TRADITIONAL MELODIC MINOR

Another alteration of the pure natural minor scale is the *traditional melodic minor* scale. This scale uses a raised 6th and 7th scale degree when ascending and lowers them when descending, improving the natural flow of a melodic line. Since the notes change depending on the direction of movement, it would be impractical to analyze this scale for chords and modes.

Fig. 3.3. Traditional Melodic Minor Scale

The *real* or *jazz* melodic minor scale is the same as the ascending traditional melodic minor scale, but the descending form is the same as the ascending form.

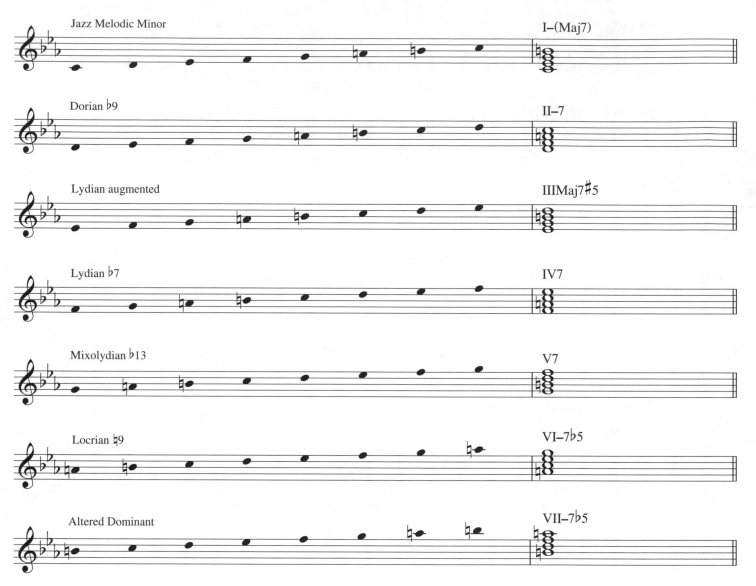

Fig. 3.4. Jazz Melodic Minor Scale

All of these scales and modes are important to understand, and it's a long-term commitment to memorize them in all keys.

USING MODES OF MINOR SCALES

Composers, arrangers, and improvisers make use of all forms of the minor scales. There are many choices available, and it is common to move from one minor mode to another during the course of a solo. For example, the I chord could be interpreted as I minor 7 if we are thinking pure natural minor, or it could be I minor 6 if we were thinking of jazz melodic minor. In figure 3.5, I have interpreted the I chord as minor 7, minor 6, and minor/major 7, implying pure natural, Dorian, and jazz melodic minor modes, respectively.

Fig. 3.5. Solo Using Modes of Minor

As you become more familiar with the musical language, consider the lead sheet a road map to the song, but there are always many possible ways to arrive at a destination other than the initial direction.

Let's begin by taking a few of the more commonly used modes from above and applying them to a progression. We'll use a minor key II–7♭5 V7(♭9, ♭13) I progression and apply the Locrian mode, the Mixolydian ♭9, ♭13 mode, and Aeolian or Dorian mode. This progression is extremely common, and learning to play the available scales will make it much easier to navigate when you experience it within the context of a song.

a. Progression in C Minor

TRACK 13

b. Progression in G Minor

TRACK 14

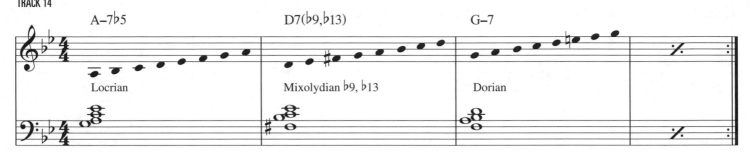

Fig. 3.6. Chord Scales in C Minor and G Minor

PRACTICE

Practice these II V I's slowly and carefully, as outlined. If you are playing chords along with the scales, make sure you match the harmony by applying the correct tensions to each voicing. (Don't voice a chord with tension 9 if you are practicing a chord scale with ♭9 or ♯9.)

1. Practice playing each scale from root to root ascending.
2. Practice playing each scale from root to root descending.
3. Practice improvising freely using the chosen chord scales.

JAZZ MELODIC MINOR SCALE

The jazz melodic scale is another great resource for harmony and melodies. Let's focus on some different choices for our II V I progression using only modes from jazz melodic.

1. Practice playing each scale from root to root ascending.
2. Practice playing each scale from root to root descending.
3. Practice improvising freely using the chosen chord scales.

Listen carefully to the differences between the first set of chord scales and the second. They both are quite functional, giving you many possible options for improvisation.

II–7♭5 Locrian Natural 9, V7 Altered, I Minor/Major 7

a. Key of C Minor

TRACK 15

b. Key of E Minor

TRACK 16

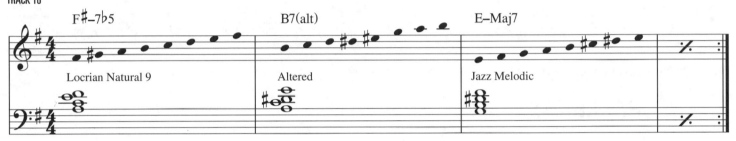

Fig. 3.7. Locrian ♮9 II–7♭5

TRACK 17

Many styles of music use progressions that move between the related major and minor key signature. Look at the progression and its analysis below. I have labeled two options of chord scales for the relative minor progression.

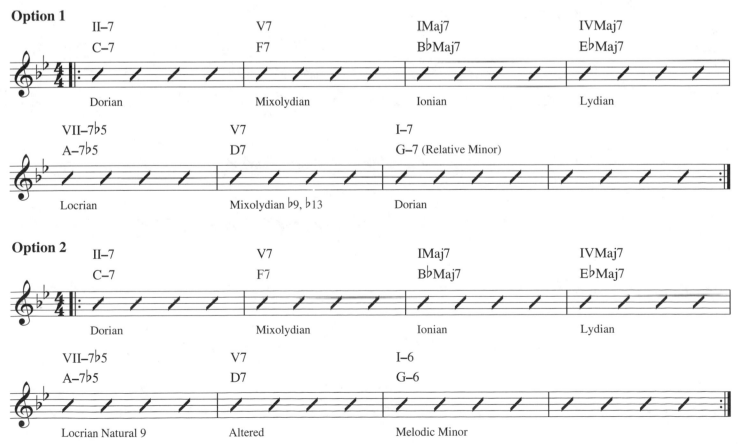

Fig. 3.8. Chords from Modes

Using option 1 and then option 2, practice the following.

1. Chord scales root-to-root ascending.
2. Chord scales descending root to root.
3. Review exercises from earlier chapters.
4. Freely improvise.

Here is the same progression to practice in the key of G major/E minor.

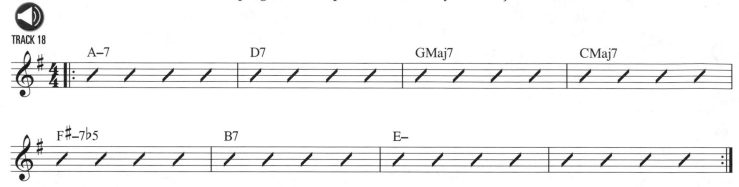

Fig. 3.9. Progression in G Major/E Minor

CHALLENGE!

Figures 3.10 and 3.11 are major and minor II V I progressions moving through all keys. Apply the modes we have worked on in chapters 2 and 3 to these progressions using the included play along.

1. Practice playing each scale from root to root ascending.
2. Practice playing each scale from root to root descending.
3. Practice improvising freely.

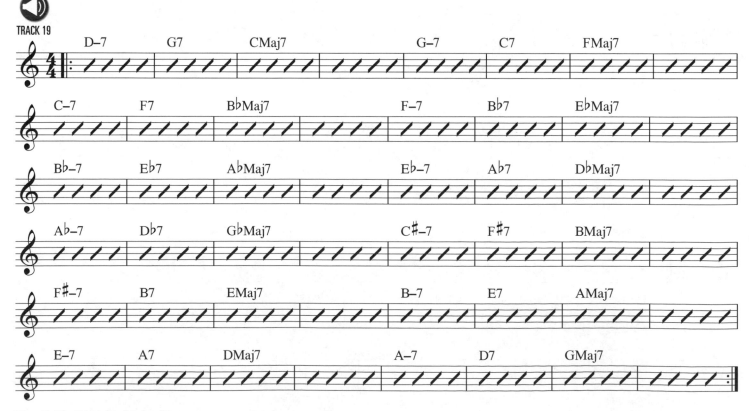

Fig. 3.10. II V I for Major Keys

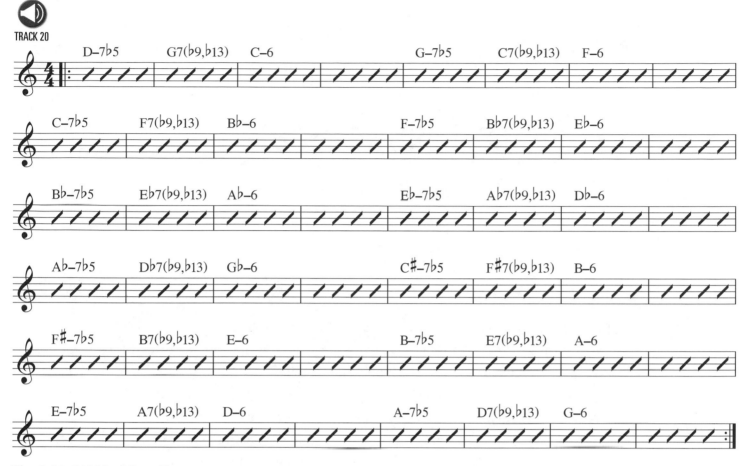

Fig. 3.11. II V I for Minor Keys

PRACTICE

Practice the fingering exercises in appendix B for modes of the Lydian ♭7, Locrian natural 9, and altered scales.

CHAPTER 4

The Blues Scale

Blues: A troublesome emotion. This is the first definition in the new *Harvard Dictionary of Music.* Before ever playing the scale that is associated with the blues, we might expect some dissonance and tension!

The blues is a genre of music that started in the late 1800s or early 1900s but has permeated, at some level, into almost all styles of music including pop, rock, r&b, gospel, jazz, and country. In addition to the styles that borrow from it, there are many subset styles of blues including Delta blues, Chicago blues, Detroit blues, Kansas City blues, and others.

BLUES SCALE

Because of its use in such a wide variety of styles, practicing and applying blues scales provides a great source of musical vocabulary. Figure 4.1 shows the C blues scale analyzed in relation to the major scale.

As you play and listen to the scale, you will probably hear the "troublesome emotions" that the scale has been used to produce. The blues scale has so-called "avoid" notes and dissonance as part of its construction, so forget about the rules; it's all about knowing when and how to break them!

Fig. 4.1. C Blues Scale

The typical form of a blues song is twelve bars, and a unique aspect of its harmony is that the I, IV, and V chords are played as *dominant* chords. A simple 12-bar blues in the key of G is shown below.

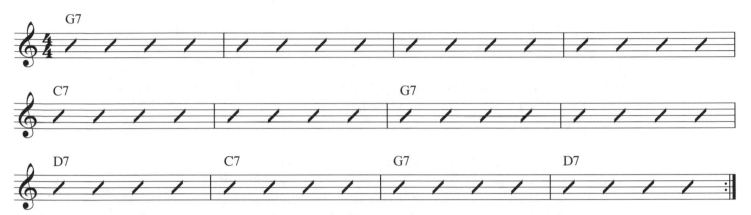

Fig. 4.2. 12-Bar Blues in G

While practicing scales up and down prepares us for using them in a song, the rhythm, phrasing, and dynamics are what really create a musical statement. Musicians often practice scales *and* phrases to develop the language of a particular style.

Three phrases created from the G blues scale are shown in figure 4.3. Practice them until you can comfortably play them from memory. Play using a swing feel.

Fig. 4.3. Three 1-Bar Blues Phrases in G

TIPS FOR MEMORIZING

Memorization occurs on three levels:

First, be able to hear the sound of what you are memorizing, so you can sing or hum the sound without touching an instrument.

Second, sense the movement that is about to happen in your hand when you play the phrase. Imagining the sound should create an image of the physical sensation of playing it.

Third, understand theoretically what you are playing. Think about what key you are in, what scale you are using, and all of the note and chord relationships. This seems like a lot to consider, but if you develop a complete understanding of the music, you will be able to create exactly the sounds you want when you improvise.

Imagine only knowing a few words of a foreign language, and being in the middle of a country where it is spoken, trying to communicate with the locals. It's the same with music, except you are in the middle of a chord progression! You don't want to have a limited vocabulary in either situation. Studying the music deeply will allow you to say what you want.

TRACK 21

EXERCISE 4.1. BLUES PHRASE CALL-AND-RESPONSE

Once you are comfortable playing the G blues scale and the phrases in figure 4.3, practice them as outlined using the play-along track 21. (Track 22 demonstrates a possible solution.) Each time through the form, you will alternate playing a phrase and resting for a measure, in measures 2, 4, 6, 8, 10, and 12, as shown in figure 4.4:

1. Play phrase 1.
2. Play phrase 2.
3. Play phrase 3.
4. Alternate playing phrase 1 and phrase 2.
5. Alternate playing all three phrases.
6. Alternate playing each written phrase and your own improvised phrase. Feel free to vary the given phrases slightly.
7. Improvise freely throughout the form.

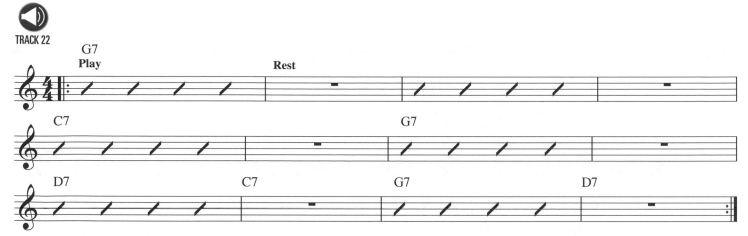

Fig. 4.4. Blues Practice

CALL-AND-RESPONSE

The call-and-response approach presented here is a common practice technique. It works well to present a musical idea and develop it over the course of a solo. As you can hear, with a little vocabulary, we can build a very musical solo.

MAJOR BLUES SCALE

Let's look at another option with the blues scale. There are two ways of describing it. I will call it the major blues scale, but it is sometimes called the *relative minor* blues scale. Either way, it adds to our vocabulary.

Analyze the scale in figure 4.5. Without any musical relationship to reference it against, it looks like an E blues scale (which it is). E is the relative minor of G, and the relative-minor blues scale works quite well on a G blues.

Fig. 4.5. E Blues Scale

If we examine this scale starting from the second note (G), the result could be labeled as a G *major* blues scale.

Fig. 4.6. G Major Blues Scale

Either way you look at it, the notes are the same. In this book, I'll refer to the two scales as the blues scale and the major blues scale. The major blues scale has less dissonant notes when played against the I7 chord. Notice that it includes many chord tones and natural tensions. Only the ♯9 is rather dissonant.

Fig. 4.7. G Blues and Major Blues Scales

EXERCISE 4.2. MAJOR BLUES PHRASE CALL-AND-RESPONSE

Let's practice major-blues-scale phrases using the same call-and-response approach as in exercise 4.1.

Fig. 4.8. Three 1-Bar Phrases of the G Major Blues Scale

Notice that there are a few spots where the major blues scale sounds out of place over the blues progression. When played over the IV7 chord, the 4th note (B natural) is the major 7th, which clashes with the flat 7th of the chord. You may decide to avoid that note during the IV7 chord.

You can freely use either blues scale while soloing over the blues. Phrases can be connected that start on one scale and end on the other. Along with the blues or major blues scale, try using the Mixolydian mode or some of the other dominant chord scales we have worked on so far. When playing the blues scales, you will apply the blues scale of the key (G major or G blues scale in figures 4.2 and 4.4). When using other dominant chord scales, use the root of the dominant chord as the source of the scale (G, C, and D Mixolydian in figures 4.2 and 4.4).

TRACK 21

EXERCISE 4.3. MAJOR BLUES SCALE PRACTICE

Practice the following with the play-along track 21.

1. Play the tonic blues scale ascending for two octaves and then descending for two octaves over the blues form.

2. Play the tonic major blues scale ascending for two octaves and descending for two octaves over the blues form.

3. Play the Mixolydian scale for each chord, root to root, ascending for one chorus then descending for the next chorus.

4. Alternate between blues and major-blues scales using the given phrases first, then improvising your own.

5. Compose six phrases of your own, based on the blues scales, and write them down in musical notation. Practice your original phrases with the play-along track.

TRACK 23

Track 23 is a demonstration of practice exercises 1, 2, and 3.

WRITE YOUR OWN BLUES PHRASES

Supplement all of the examples I give you with your own ideas, which you should write down in your music notebook. As a developing improviser, creating your own phrases helps you to develop a unique voice as a soloist. Beyond writing your own ideas down, as you listen to your favorite recordings, figure out some of the phrases you like best, and write those down as well. Develop your vocabulary by practicing all of them in time and in every key.

MORE PHRASES FOR PRACTICE

Here are five more G blues phrases of varying length for you to practice. As with all of the scales and exercises, eventually you will want to master them in all keys. Start with one phrase, and work it through the keys one at a time. You will find that practicing studies in all keys gets easier and easier, the more you do it.

Fig. 4.9. Blues Licks

BLUES FORM VARIATIONS

There are countless variations on the blues progressions. Below I have included a minor blues and a jazz blues with some suggested scales to practice in addition to the blues scale of the key. Notice that in the case of the minor blues, the major blues scale is not a good option.

TRACK 24

Minor Blues Form

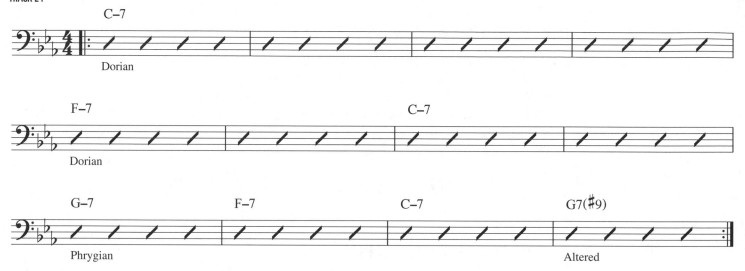

Fig. 4.10. C Minor 12-Bar Blues

TRACK 25

Jazz Blues Form

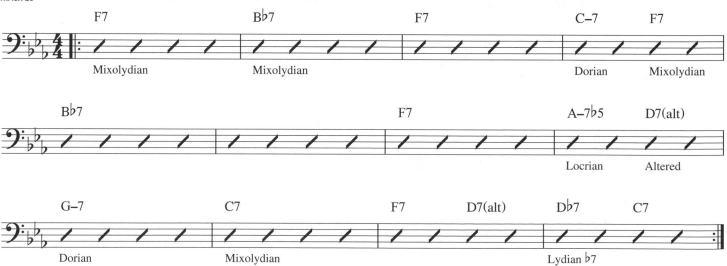

Fig. 4.11. 12-Bar Jazz Blues

PRACTICE

Practice the fingering exercises in appendix C for modes of blues scales.

CHAPTER 5

Developing Musical Phrases: Approach Notes

Until now, we have practiced soloing using notes from a specific chord scale combined with the targeting of chord tones (root, 3rd, and 5th). What about notes not in the scale? Are there ways of using those as well?

The answer is yes; every note in the chromatic scale has a use.

Notes that are not included in a chosen chord scale can be utilized in a few ways.

1. As neighbor tones.
2. As passing tones.
3. When intentionally playing "outside" the chord changes.

PLAYING OUTSIDE

Playing "outside" means intentionally playing scales and patterns that are in direct opposition to the supplied chord changes, from a theoretical viewpoint. For example: playing a C♯ Dorian mode when the given chord symbol is C–7 would be "outside." We will save this more advanced approach for later in the book and focus now on neighbor and passing tones.

Types of non-chord tones used in melody include passing tones, neighbor tones, and approach notes. Each of these labels can be broken down further into even more specifics based on their usage, but we will focus on their general application to our improvisation.

These notes are used to embellish chord tones either chromatically or diatonically, from above or below. We can use a single note or combine notes to create a wide variety of options. Some common examples are shown in figure 5.1, targeting the root, 3rd, and 5th of C major and C minor triads.

1. Chromatic approach from below.
2. Scalar approach from above.
3. Double approach using scalar from above and chromatic from below.
4. Double approach using chromatic from below and scalar from above.
5. Combined approach variation.
6. Combined approach variation using chromatic from above and below.

Fig. 5.1. C Major and Minor Approach Notes

Notice that the choice of chord scale will determine the specifics of your scalar approach notes. For example: the approach note to the 5th from above in C minor would be A natural in Dorian mode and an A♭ in Aeolian mode.

These embellishments can be applied to any type of chord, and they can provide variation to an otherwise lifeless line. The example in figure 5.2 shows a simple melody outlining the chord tones of a C7 chord.

Fig. 5.2. C7 Outline

If we apply some approach notes, this same melody becomes something more forward moving and exciting.

Fig. 5.3. C7 Outline with Approach Notes

PRACTICE

Let's practice embellishments using a progression we worked on in chapter 3. Track 26 is a demonstration of approach notes.

Practice the progression using the following methods.

1. Chromatic from below to root.
2. Scale from above to root.
3. Combined chromatic from below to scale from above to root.
4. Combined scale from above to chromatic from below to root.
5. Repeat steps (1) to (4) targeting the 3rd chord tone.
6. Repeat steps (1) to (4) targeting the 5th chord tone.
7. Repeat steps (1) to (4) targeting the 7th chord tone.

TRACK 18   TRACK 26

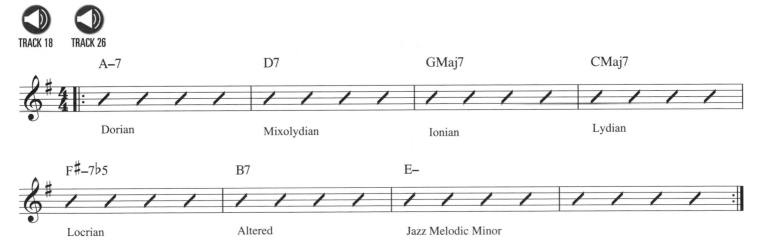

Fig. 5.4. Progression

Depending on the rhythms you choose, you can approach more than one chord tone per measure, as shown in figure 5.5. Try incorporating these into an improvised solo of your own.

TRACK 27

Fig. 5.5. Common Jazz Progression

CHROMATIC PASSING TONES

We can use chromatic notes to connect consecutive notes from a single chord scale or to help us shift between chord scales as shown below.

Fig. 5.6. Chromatic Passing Tones Used with a Mixolydian Chord Scale

Fig. 5.7. Chromatic Passing Tones between Dorian, Mixolydian, and Ionian Chord Scales in a II V I Progression

II V I

Because the II V I progression is extremely common, let's use it to practice putting together some melodic phrases (also know as "lines") that make use of our chord scales and some chromatic passing tones.

Practice the phrases below one at a time following the key area charts in figures 5.11 and 5.12. Line 1 is demonstrated on track 29.

TRACK 29

Fig. 5.8. Line 1. Starting on root.

Fig. 5.9. Line 2. Starting on 3rd.

Fig. 5.10. Line 3. Starting on 5th.

TRACK 28

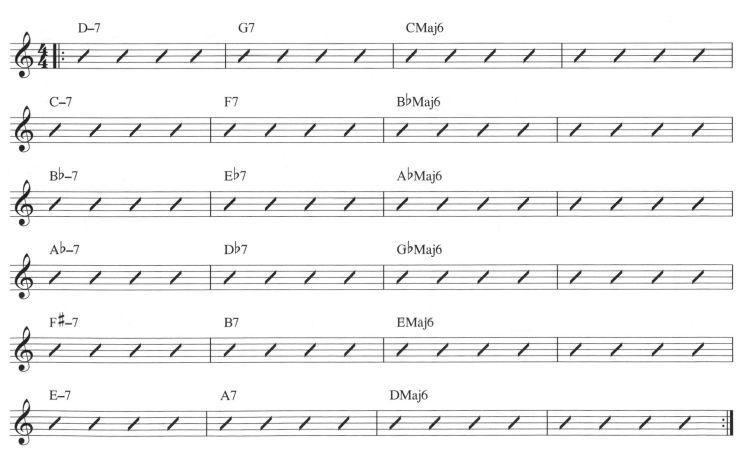

Fig. 5.11. II V I Descending Whole Steps Starting in the Key of C Major

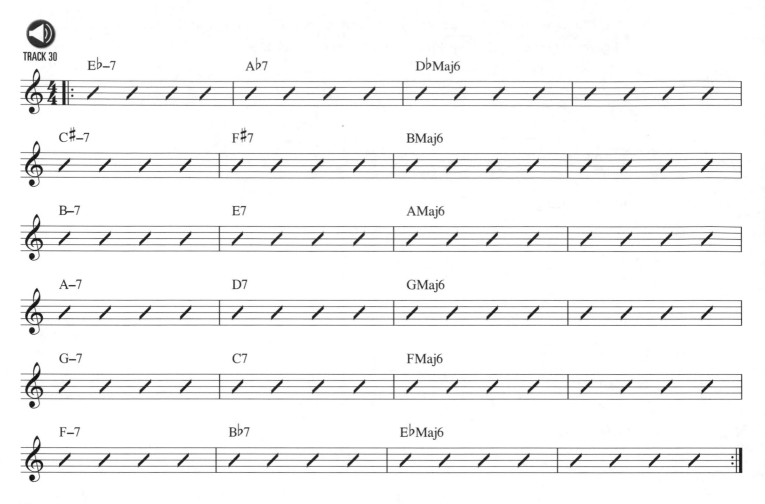

Fig. 5.12. II V I Descending Whole Steps Starting in the Key of D♭ Major

We can also use similar phrases with our minor key area. Let's use the melodic minor modes and apply the same linear shape. Line 1 is demonstrated on track 33.

Fig. 5.13. Minor Key Line 1. Starting on root.

Fig. 5.14. Minor Key Line 2. Starting on 3rd.

Fig. 5.15. Minor Key Line 3. Starting on 5th.

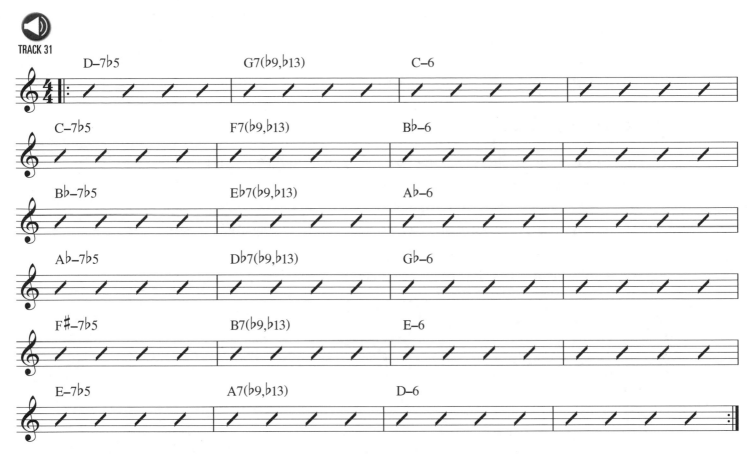

Fig. 5.16. II V I Descending Whole Steps Starting in the Key of C Minor

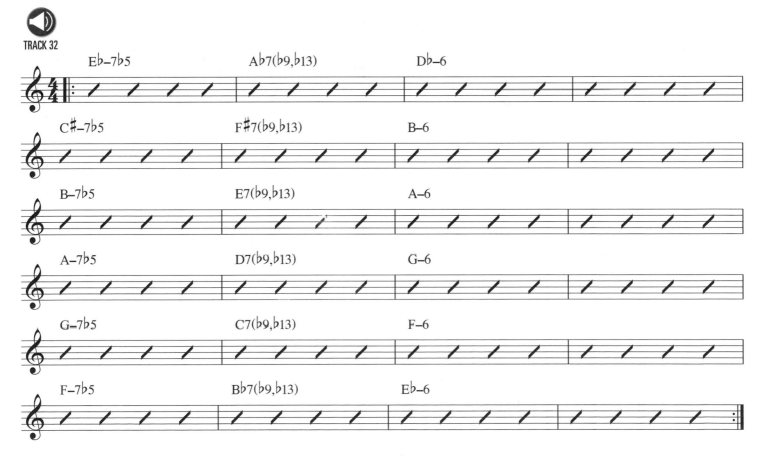

Fig. 5.17. II V I Descending Whole Steps Starting in the Key of D♭ Minor

When you feel comfortable playing the major and minor phrases, use the play along to practice moving from key to key in time. Because all of these lines end with a single note, try improvising a short phrase on the I chord before moving to the next line after you have mastered them as written.

BEBOP SCALES

Musicians often utilize chromatic passing tones in their playing, and there are some specific examples that are called "bebop" scales.

Bebop scales are 8-note variations of other scales that add a chromatic passing tone between two chord tones. You can use these starting from any scale degree, aiming for the downbeat when coming in on a chord tone, and the upbeat when starting on any passing tone to maintain their sound.

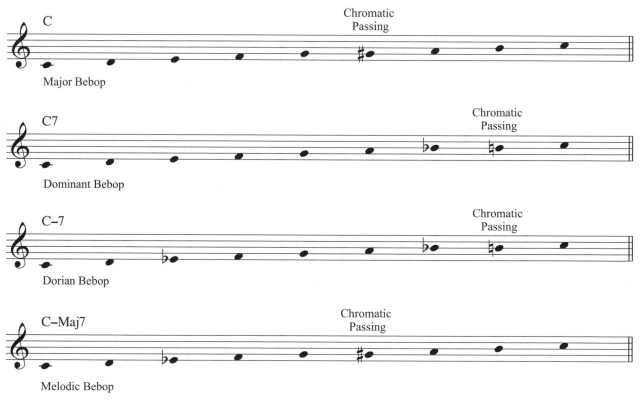

Fig. 5.18. Bebop Scales

PRACTICE

Practice the bebop scales with the included play-along progressions or with any lead sheets you are working with. Here are a few ways to approach practicing them:

1. Starting on the root on the downbeat.
2. Starting on the 3rd on the downbeat.
3. Starting on the 5th on the downbeat.
4. Starting on the 9th on the upbeat of 1.
5. Starting on the 11th on the upbeat of 1.

Figure 5.19 shows how bebop scales can be used in a solo.

TRACK 34

Fig. 5.19. Bebop Scale Solo

CHAPTER 6

Symmetrical Scales

Symmetrical scales are created from intervallic patterns that repeat within the octave. These include the whole tone, diminished, augmented, and chromatic scales.

WHOLE TONE SCALE

The *whole tone scale* is a series of whole steps.

Fig. 6.1. C Whole Tone Scale

Notice that the whole tone scale is made up of only six notes. There are only two whole tone scales, in terms of pitch content (and discounting enharmonic spellings), which you can find by beginning on C and on C♯. The C whole tone scale (figure 6.1) contains exactly the same notes as whole tone scales beginning on D, E, F♯, G♯, and A♯.

The C♯ whole tone scale (figure 6.2) contains exactly the same notes as D♯, F, G, A, and B whole tone scales.

Fig. 6.2. C♯ Whole Tone Scale

The whole tone scale can be used over an augmented triad or a dominant 7♯5 chord.

EXERCISE 6.1. WHOLE TONE PHRASE PRACTICE

Practice these four solo phrases built from the whole tone scale. The first three are in the context of a II V I progression, and the fourth is set in a progression using secondary dominants. Figure 6.6 is shown with a resolution to a major 7 chord after three measures, but the practice figure 6.7 is a continuous succession of dominant chords. Notice that the given chord voicing supports the whole tone scale with natural 9 and ♯5 (enharmonically ♭13).

PRACTICE TIPS

Practice each musical phrase slowly until you can play it without looking at the music. Make sure you understand each note's relationship to the chord. Once memorized, transpose the phrase to all keys, and practice each using play-along tracks 19, 28, and 30 for figures 6.3, 6.4, and 6.5, and track 35 for 6.6 using a dominant cycle 5 progression. Write your own phrases built from the whole tone scale in your notebook, and listen for the sound of whole tone scales in recorded solos for transcription.

Fig. 6.3. Whole Tone Phrase 1. For II V I progressions.

Fig. 6.4. Whole Tone Phrase 2. For II V I progressions.

Fig. 6.5. Whole Tone Phrase 3. For II V I progressions.

Fig. 6.6. Whole Tone Phrase 4. For cycle V progression.

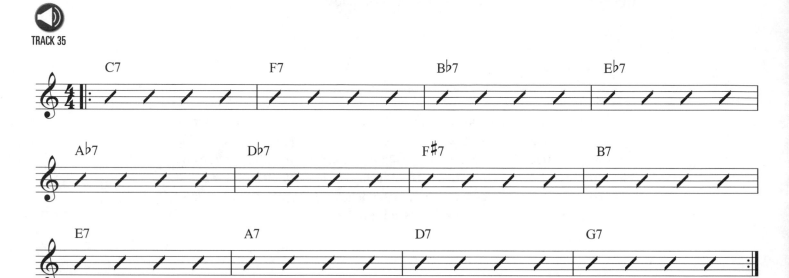

Fig. 6.7. Cycle 5 Dominant Chord Practice

DIMINISHED SCALES

The diminished scales are created by alternating whole steps and half steps. The pattern results in an 8-note scale, and because of this, is also known as the "octatonic" scale.

There are two types of diminished scales: one starting with a half step and one starting with a whole step. Three sets of pitches are possible using these patterns.

Half/Whole

The half-step/whole-step diminished scale is most commonly used with dominant 7 chords, and it yields a number of interesting pitch combinations. It includes all of the chord tones: root, 3rd, 5th, ♭7, and tensions ♭9, ♯9, ♯11, and 13.

Fig. 6.8. C Half/Whole Diminished Scale

There are three possible starting points for the half/whole-diminished scale before notes repeat; you can find them by starting on C, C♯, and D.

Each half/whole-diminished scale contains four dominant 7 chords separated by minor 3rds. For example, a C half/whole diminished scale contains the notes of C7, E♭7, F♯7, and A7. Therefore, any phrase created using the C half/whole diminished scale can be played with a C7, E♭7, F♯7, or A7 chord.

Fig. 6.9. Four Dominant Chords from C Half/Whole Diminished

The diminished scale can be used to create some very interesting phrases with dominant 7th chords. Pay careful attention to the fact that the scale contains ♭9 and ♯9, ♯11, and natural 5 and 13; this combination of notes shifts between sounding altered to sounding Mixolydian.

EXERCISE 6.2. HALF/WHOLE DIMINISHED SCALE PHRASES

Let's apply the half/whole diminished scale to some phrases. In figure 6.10, notice the tensions applied to the chord voicing are in alignment with the use of the half/whole-diminished scale. Practice the scale using the V7 to I progression as shown in all keys, being careful to apply the correct tensions to your LH voicing.

Fig. 6.10. Chords with Tensions under Half/Whole Scale

Memorize each phrase of figure 6.10 through 6.14 one at a time, and transpose them to every key. Use the appropriate play-along II V I tracks (19, 28, 30) as accompaniments for all of your II V I practicing. As you work on lead sheets, apply the lines freely while practicing your solos. Once you have mastered these lines, write your own in your notebook. Eventually you will have pages of musical lines to draw inspiration from.

Fig. 6.11. Melodic Practice Example 1

Chromatic
Approach

Fig. 6.12. Melodic Practice Example 2

Figure 6.13 is simply climbing up the diminished scale in thirds and resolving
to the I chord.

Fig. 6.13. Climbing Diminished Scale in Thirds

Figure 6.14 is a 4-note pattern lowered repeatedly by minor 3rds into a
resolution. Notice that the pattern starts with each root of the four possible
major/minor/diminished triads and then resolves where it started on the 5th of
the I chord. Try playing this pattern on the dominant cycle 5 progression using
play-along track 35.

Fig. 6.14. Descending Half/Whole Pattern

DIMINISHED SCALE AND UPPER-STRUCTURE TRIADS

Another way to create interesting chord voicings and linear phrases is to use structures other than the primary structures (i.e., root triad) that are contained within the harmonic framework.

We can take any chord scale and make use of the diatonic triads contained within the harmony as an upper structure. Each triad will yield a unique combination of tensions and chord tones, and the secondary structure of a triad over a chord results in harmony that sounds rich and flavorful.

The diminished scale is unusually rich in these harmonies. Unlike a major scale, which yields seven diatonic chords, the diminished scale yields sixteen different triads and four dominant 7th chords. Figure 6.15 identifies all of the possible chord structures from a C half/whole diminished scale. All of them can be played as chords or as arpeggios over the original C7 chord.

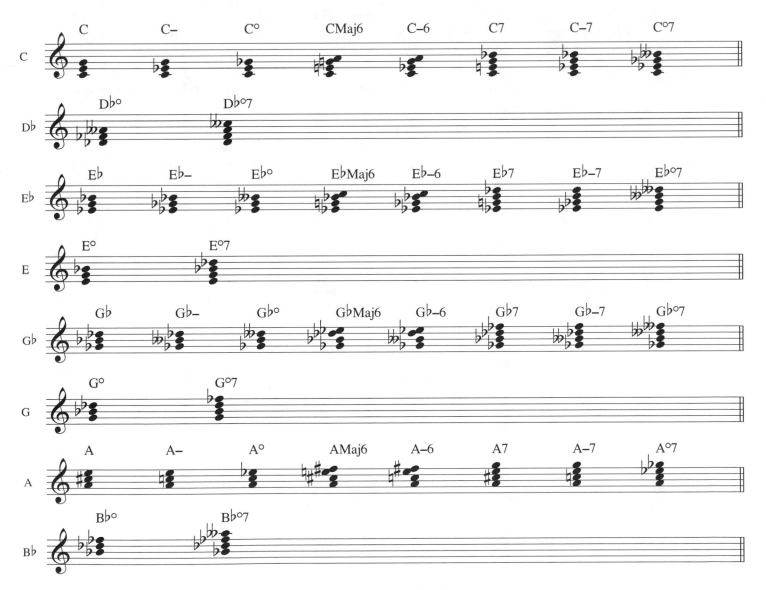

Fig. 6.15. Available Chords Derived from C Half/Whole Diminished Scale

Figure 6.16 shows some typical voicing applications of upper-structure triads found in a C half/whole diminished scale.

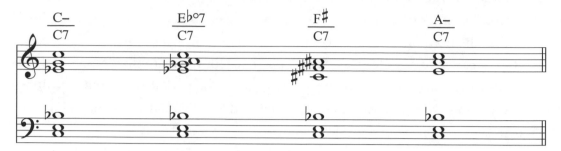

Fig. 6.16. Four Upper-Structure Triad Voicings

MAJOR 7 AND NATURAL 4

When working with a dominant 7 chord, there is only one note that does not occur in any of our dominant chord scales: the major 7. (While it exists in bebop scales, it functions there purely as a chromatic passing tone, so I don't include it harmonically.)

The other note to be careful with is the natural 4. In most cases, this note is avoided when creating upper structures for dominant 7 chords.

Figure 6.17 shows two more II V7 I progressions utilizing the half/whole-diminished scale with the dominant chords. Notice the clear use of upper structure triads. Practice these phrases in all keys using the major key II V I play-along tracks 19, 28, and 30.

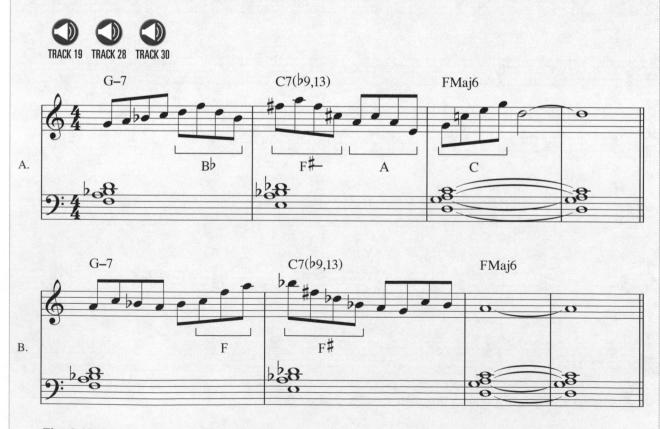

Fig. 6.17. Melodic Practice Example 3

PRACTICING UPPER-STRUCTURE TRIADS

When learning to use upper structures, study them based on the triad type and its distance from the root of the dominant chord. For example, phrase 6.17A uses an A triad at the end of the C7 chord. Since the A is the 6th scale degree of C, you could simply memorize that any major triad built on the 6th scale degree of a dominant chord is an available upper-structure triad.

Fig. 6.18. 6th Scale Degree Major Triads as Upper Structures

Also memorize what tensions and chord tones each triad includes. In the case of the A over C7 (or VI major upper-structure triad), we get tension ♭9, 13, and chord tone 3. See figure 6.19 for a list of possible upper-structure triads and their associated chord scales.

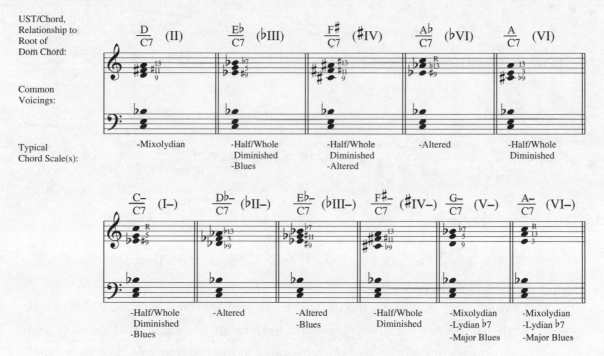

Fig. 6.19. Major and Minor Upper-Structure Triads

WHOLE/HALF DIMINISHED

The whole/half version of the diminished scale is commonly played with diminished chords.

Fig. 6.20. Whole/Half Diminished Scale

In most cases, diminished chords are used as passing chords to create a chromatic bass motion. Notice that the diminished passing chords are functioning similarly to a secondary dominant with ♭9 in typical usage. Play the two progressions below.

Fig. 6.21. C♯°7 Passing Chord (Enharmonic Spelling)

Fig. 6.22. A7(♭9,13) Passing Chord

The only difference between C♯°7 and A7(♭9,13) is the bass note; the passing diminished chord version creates a chromatic ascending line to D–7. As we have learned, you would play the C♯ whole/half scale on the C♯°7, and A half/whole scale on the A7(♭9,13), but the notes are exactly the same, just starting from different points. These two progressions are interchangeable, from a soloist's standpoint.

PRACTICE

EXERCISE 6.3. WHOLE/HALF DIMINISHED SCALE PHRASE PRACTICE

Using the common progression in figure 6.23, practice each indicated chord scale using eighth notes starting from the root of each chord ascending, and then descending. Then transpose the exercise to all keys. In conjunction with practicing the scales, improvise freely and try to incorporate new ideas into your solo.

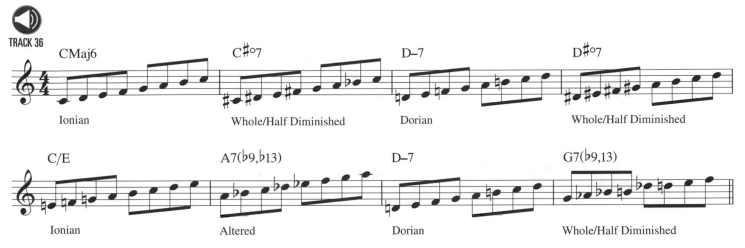

Fig. 6.23. Diminished Passing Chord Scales in C

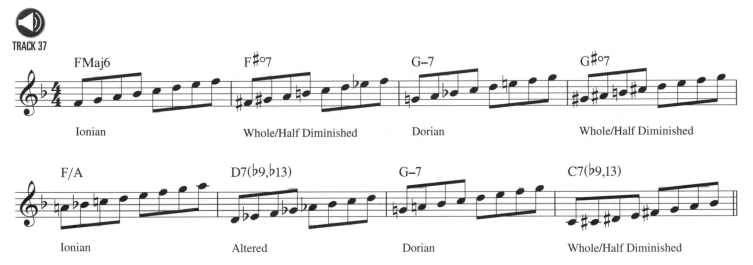

Fig. 6.24. Diminished Passing Chord Scales in F

CHOOSING SCALES

It's important to remember that we are dealing with styles of music that include improvisation, so lead sheets are only giving general directions. For example, the choice to use half/whole diminished or Lydian ♭7 on a certain dominant chord is greatly a matter of taste. This choice is made within the context of the chord symbol on the lead sheet, which may or may not indicate specific tensions, combined with the harmonic function of the chord and its relationship to the melody.

During solos, there are more possibilities, because it is not necessary to support the original melody. We may find ourselves venturing out into new areas of the song. How far you travel is up to the soloist and the band.

While there are no clear-cut rules when improvising, the chart below shows directional tendencies using the most commonly applied scales. The specific way you apply the chord scale will influence how well the resolution works.

V7(9,13) tends to resolve to major.

(Mixolydian)

(Lydian ♭7)

Fig. 6.25. Dominant Scales with Major Resolution

V7(♭9,♭13) tends to resolve to minor.

(Altered Scale)

(5th Mode of Harmonic Minor)

Fig. 6.26. Dominant Scales with Minor Resolution

V7(9,♭13) can resolve to major or minor.

(5th Mode of Melodic Minor)

(5th Mode of Melodic Minor)

Fig. 6.27. Dominant Scales with Major or Minor Resolution

V7#5(9) tends to resolve to major.

(Whole Tone)

Fig. 6.28. Dominant (Whole Tone) Scale with Major Resolution

V7 (♭9, 13) resolves to major or minor.

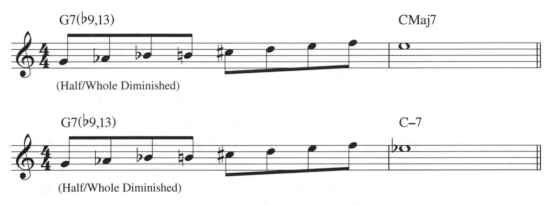

(Half/Whole Diminished)

(Half/Whole Diminished)

Fig. 6.29. Dominant (Half/Whole Diminished) Scale with Major and Minor Resolution

Because the half/whole diminished scale contains a natural 13, you might think it suggests a smoother resolution when used as a V7 resolving to a major chord. If you analyze the harmony, natural 13 (A on a C7) is the 3rd of the I chord (A on an FMaj7).

On the other hand, the first five notes of the scale are identical to the altered scale, and it can resolve smoothly to minor. Figure 6.29 shows examples of the half/whole diminished scale resolving to major and minor. Does either sound wrong to you?

Again, choice of scale is subjective, and the possibilities are endless—including the combination of multiple scales. The more comfortable you are with your ability to control your choices, the more likely the choices you make will create the most musical result. Every note is possible!

CHAPTER 7

Beyond the Changes

While some songs specify many chord changes and shifting key signatures, others are written with very few chords, providing minimal harmonic change for the soloist. Simpler progressions are common in many styles of music, including modal jazz, funk, fusion, reggae, and rock. But just because the prescribed harmonies are simple doesn't mean that you have to always keep strictly within the boundaries of what's written. This chapter covers a lot of techniques that will take years of practice to fully integrate into your playing. Practice each using the included play alongs as well as integrating them into the music you are most interested in.

THINKING MODALLY

While we generally consider songs as being in either a major or a minor key, we now know there are many modes of those scales available to use as a basis for writing and improvising. Modal songs often have very few chord changes; the harmonic effect comes from the overall sound of the mode rather than specifically functioning chords.

For example, Dorian mode is used commonly for composition. Miles Davis's "So What" and Freddie Hubbard's "Little Sunflower" are good examples of Dorian songs that have relatively few chord changes.

You can identify a song's mode by a number of factors:
1. The key signature. A modal key signature reflects the major scale from which it is derived. Key signatures for D Dorian, E Phrygian, F Lydian, G Mixolydian, and A Aeolian would have no sharps or flats because they are modes of C major.
2. Characteristic note. Each mode has a characteristic note that helps indicate the song is written in that mode. Each mode's characteristic note is shown in figure 7.1. If you are trying to imply a mode during your solo, make frequent use of these notes.

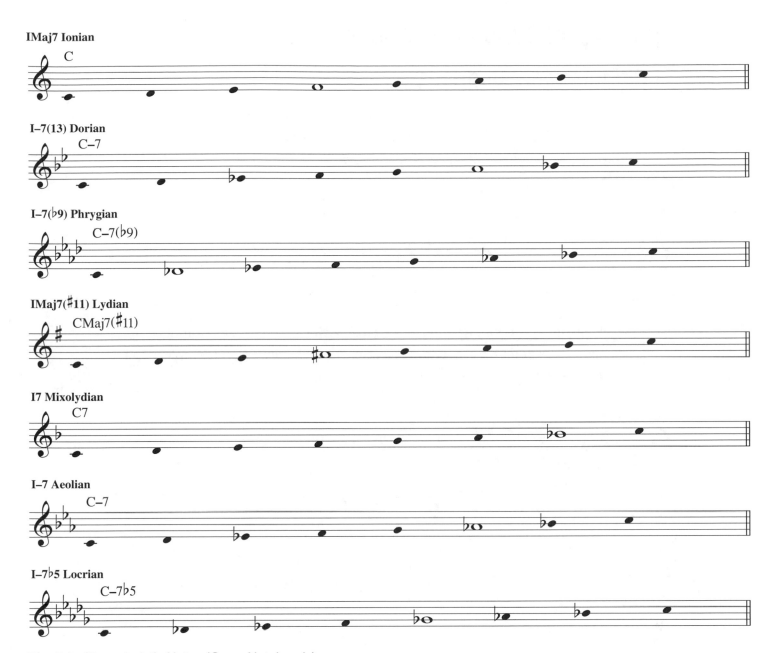

Fig. 7.1. Characteristic Notes (Open Noteheads)

3. Frequently played bass note representing the tonic. Repeating the tonic chord's bass note helps to identify the mode's harmonic center.

In some ways, learning to solo over complex chord progressions is easier than soloing over simple ones because when there are so many harmonic shifts, even basic ideas can sound interesting. With modal music, or any of the styles featuring little harmonic movement, the challenge is to create interesting solo lines when we have been initially given little to work with.

The following ideas may not work on every song that you are improvising on, but will give you some possibilities on how to expand on the concepts we have already learned. These methods potentially can be applied to any song style, not just modal songs.

SHIFTING TO PARALLEL MODES/SCALES
Static Harmonic Region

One way to create an interesting solo is to shift from the original mode into a parallel mode. To begin practicing this, we'll use a simple D Dorian vamp as the starting point to all of our examples, as shown below.

TRACK 38 TRACK 39

Fig. 7.2. D Minor Modal Vamp

Even though D Dorian would be the most obvious choice for a D minor chord, any mode has potential for creating an interesting change. As an example, apply the following modes to figure 7.2:

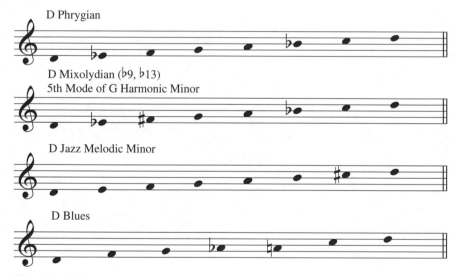

Fig. 7.3. Various Modes in D

Using play-along track 38, practice soloing using each mode. After concentrating on a single mode, try weaving melodic lines that shift from one mode to another. Listen to track 39 for an example of shifting modes during a solo over this vamp.

Changing Harmonies

Here is another vamp, but this time using two chords.

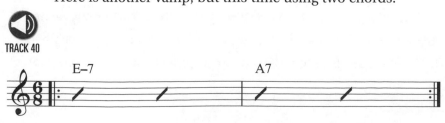

TRACK 40

Fig. 7.4. Vamp with Two Chords

Look at the following pairs of chord scales to be used with the progression.

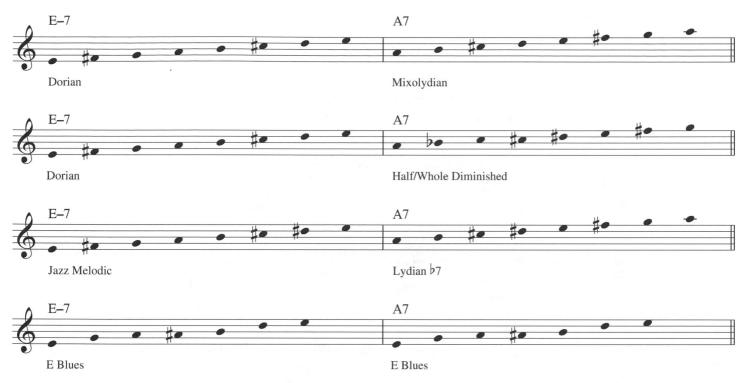

Fig. 7.5. E– to A7 Chord Scales

Using play-along track 40, practice soloing using each mode combination as outlined. After concentrating on the specific pairing of each mode, try weaving melodic lines that shift between any of the appropriate modes.

TIP: QUARTAL VOICINGS

One of the characteristics of modal playing is the use of chord voicings derived from intervals of fourths. Rather than thinking of these chords as functional I, II, III chords, etc., they simply support the sound of the mode. Figure 7.6 shows 3-note voicings in fourths for D Dorian. You can apply this style of voicing to any mode.

D Dorian Quartal Voicings

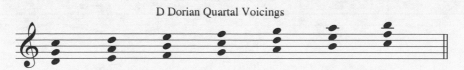

Fig. 7.6. D Dorian Quartal Voioings

PATTERNS

Music is made up of patterns; patterns in melodies, patterns of chords, rhythmic patterns, etc. Once you have mastered the scales presented in this book, then you can apply any type of pattern to them.

Practice these patterns using any scale or mode. Notice in figure 7.7 (D), the 4-note shape played rhythmically as triplets implies a polyrhythm of 3 against 4.

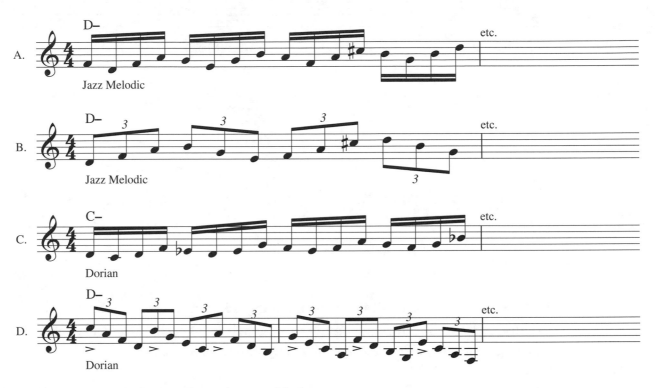

Fig. 7.7. Melodic Pattern Examples over Modes

Patterns do not need to be limited to a single chord to continue. The patterns in figure 7.8 maintain the same shape while shifting modes to accommodate chord changes. This is a great exercise and much more challenging over multiple chord changes.

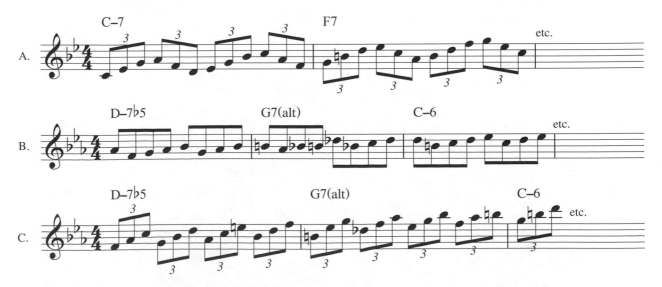

Fig. 7.8. Pattern Shapes over Chord Changes

TIP: SCALE PRACTICE

Rather than play through any scale exercise (e.g., Hanon) in a single key, choose a single exercise and play every key of any single mode. Start with all keys of a major scale, move to jazz melodic minor, then harmonic minor, and eventually all of the modes.

COMBINING SCALE PATTERNS WITH UPPER-STRUCTURE TRIADS

We can also create interesting phrases using patterns built with upper structures, and combining two or more yields some great sounding lines. There are four upper-structure triad combinations used over various types of chords shown below.

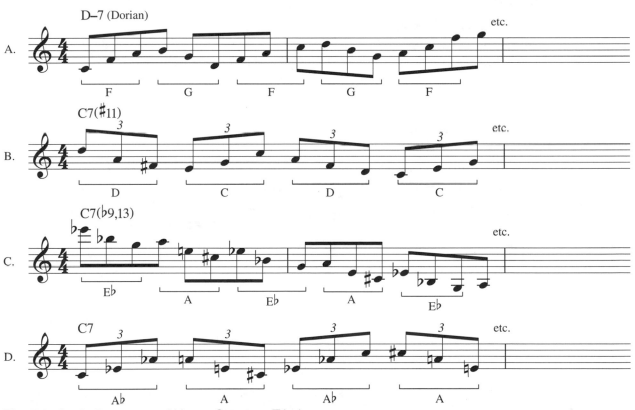

Fig. 7.9. Scale Patterns and Upper-Structure Triads

Play each phrase, and listen carefully to the sound. Make sure you clearly see where the triads are and from what chord scale they are derived. Once you feel confident with playing them in the given key, practice them in all keys. Similar to how we analyzed the upper-structure triads in chapter 6, relate the structures to the chord symbol. For example: in figure 7.9 (D), you are playing major triads based on the ♭6 and 6th scale degrees of C (A♭ triad and A triad). If you memorize them this way, it's easier to apply them to other keys.

These are just a few of hundreds of possible harmonic and rhythmic combinations, so continue to create new ones, keeping track of them in your notebook.

SCALE FRAGMENTS

We've worked with 6-, 7-, and 8-note scales in the previous lessons. One way to create a change in the sound is to use only parts of those scales, reducing the note choices to four or five, for example. Limiting the amount of notes also makes it more difficult to identify the scale, which can be an interesting approach to soloing.

Below are examples of playing scale fragments from the given chord scale over a dominant chord.

Fig. 7.10. Melodic Scale Fragments Example 1

Fig. 7.11. Melodic Scale Fragments Example 2

The solo in figure 7.12 only uses scale degrees 1, 2, 3, and 5 of each chord scale.

Fig. 7.12. Melodic Scale Fragments Example 3

The solo in figure 7.13 limits the chord scale degrees to 5, 6, 7, and 2 (tension 9).

Fig. 7.13. Melodic Scale Fragments Example 4

Using any of the modes, choose some fragmented note combinations that you find most interesting, and write them in your notebook. Label the chords they can be used with and what scale they come from. Apply them to any chord changes you are working on.

PENTATONIC SCALES

Any scale created with five notes is considered a pentatonic scale. While we looked at scale fragments from a variety of sources that had five notes, the most common pentatonic scale is shown in figure 7.14, in major and relative minor versions.

Fig. 7.14. Pentatonic Scale (Major and Minor Forms)

The pentatonic scale is a great source for melodic ideas, and there are a few options, other than using the scale based on the root of the chord you are improvising on, that work well.

Figure 7.15 shows available pentatonic scales on major, minor, and dominant chords along with each note's function. There is no difference between the major and relative minor forms of this pentatonic scale; the scales shown for D–7 could be thought of as D minor, A minor, and E minor, or F major, C major, and G major respectively.

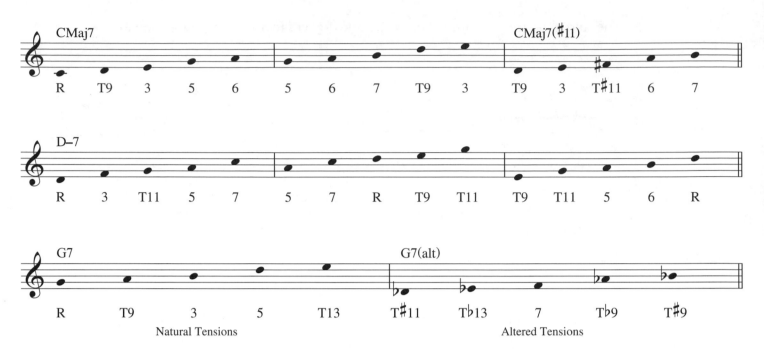

CMaj7									CMaj7($\sharp$11)				
R	T9	3	5	6	5	6	7	T9	3	T9	3	T$\sharp$11	6	7

D–7													
R	3	T11	5	7	5	7	R	T9	T11	T9	T11	5	6	R

G7						G7(alt)					
R	T9	3	5	T13	T$\sharp$11	T$\flat$13	7	T$\flat$9	T$\sharp$9

Natural Tensions   Altered Tensions

Fig. 7.15. Major and Minor Pentatonic Scales

Figure 7.16 is an example of pentatonic scales in a solo over a major key II–7 V7 I progression.

Fig. 7.16. Melodic Example of Pentatonic Scale Usage

Another interesting pentatonic scale is shown in figure 7.17. You could call this a minor 6 pentatonic scale; all of the notes are contained in the jazz melodic minor scale. It is also known as the Kumoi scale.

Fig. 7.17. Kumoi Scale

There are a number of chord types this scale can function with, as shown in figure 7.18.

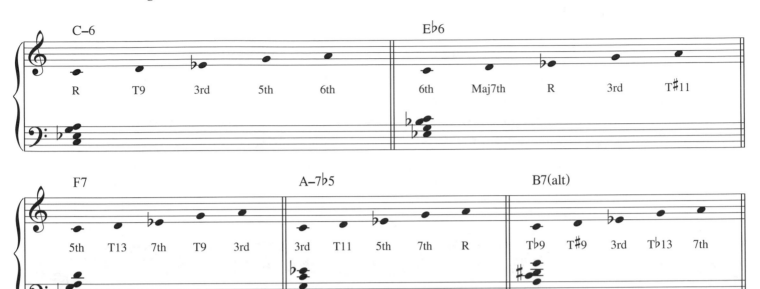

Fig. 7.18. Chord Types for C Kumoi Scale

Figure 7.19 is an example of this scale being used in a solo over a minor key II–7 V7 I progression.

Fig. 7.19. Solo Using Kumoi Scale

One way to approach memorizing these scale forms is to consider where the roots of the patterns are in relation to the chord. For example, major pentatonic scales can be played starting on the root or 5th of a major chord. They can also be played starting on the 9th if tension #11 is available. Carefully study the scale charts in figures 7.15 and 7.18, and apply these scales to any progressions you are working on.

IMPLIED HARMONY

Functional

When faced with long periods of little or no chord changes in a solo section, you can imply chord changes based on the phrases that you create that allow us to move outside of the harmonic limitations. As keyboard players, we can also further support the implied harmony with a chord voicing. As an example, given a solo section of D–7 (D Dorian), we can easily add a dominant chord functioning as the V7 or subV7 of D to create some additional tension in a solo as shown below.

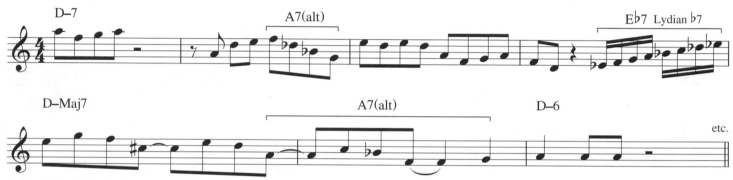

Fig. 7.20. Melodic Example Using V7 and SubV7

Notice that using the V7 altered scale and the subV7 Lydian ♭7 scale results in the same pool of note choices, since they are both from the same melodic minor scale!

Because any chord can be preceded by its dominant, by choosing a point of resolution (target chord), we can add a number of possible harmonic additions.

Using figure 7.21 as a starting point, the added V7 could be preceded by its subV7, resulting in a further departure from the original D–7 chord.

Fig. 7.21. Melodic Example Using subV7 of V7

Keep in mind a few rules of harmony to open up your choices:
1. Target chords can be preceded by their V7, subV7, or ♭VII7.
2. Any dominant chord can also be preceded by its related II–7.
3. You can change any of the above dominant chords into 7sus4 to create a different flavor.

Figure 7.22 shows two ways of adding functional harmony to a solo section with only a single chord.

Original Progression

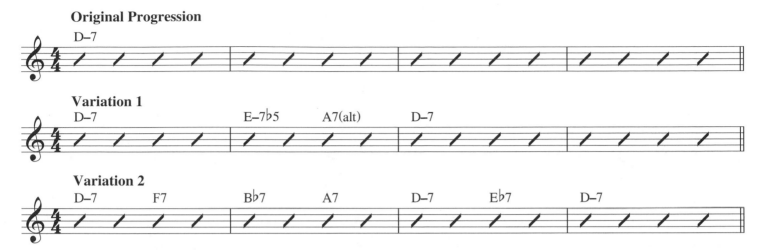

Fig. 7.22. D– Resolving Progression Variations

We can apply a similar system to songs that have regular chord movement to increase the harmonic possibilities, as shown in figure 7.23.

Original Progression

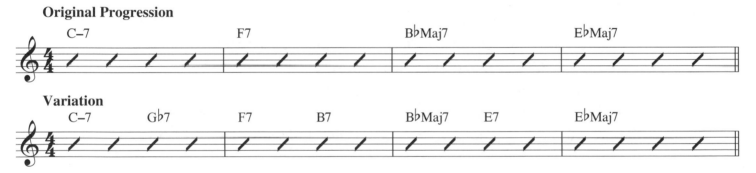

Fig. 7.23. Progression and Variation

We can also make changes to the chord progressions to create some momentary shifts in the harmonic direction. The graphic below shows a common harmonization used in jazz standards. The original form of this progression is completely diatonic to the key of A♭. By replacing the V of the tonic A♭ with a subV7 and its related II–7, we created a momentary shift that sounds like we might be in the key of D.

Original Progression

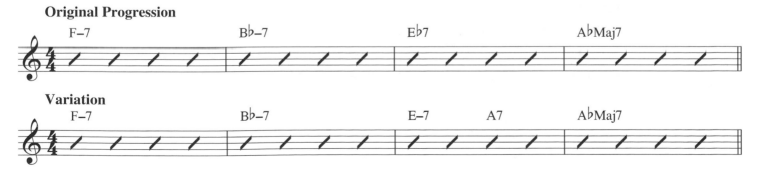

Fig. 7.24. Momentary Shift

Another example of adding harmony to a simple II V is shown below. The added II V is a half step above the original, and functionally the F♯7 is a subV7 of the original F7.

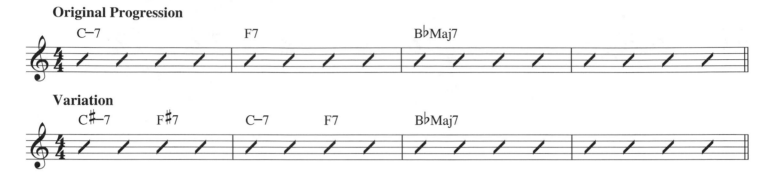

Fig. 7.25. II V Progression and Variation

INSIDE OUTSIDE

The term "inside" to most musicians refers to playing within the confines of well-established music theory. The boundary of what is "inside" or "outside" becomes a little blurry at times. When we start adding chords that were not part of the composition in a functional manner, does that cross the line into outside, or does the relationship still maintain a logical function? I will let you decide where you enter the "outside" and return to the inside, as we look at a few more ways of creating some interesting solo phrases.

Even though many of my students who are wonderful players say they don't like math, they are using it every time they play the piano. There are countless mathematical equations being performed as we create harmonic and melodic relationships, and sometimes we can use some simple math to create very interesting results.

The human brain likes patterns and structure, and one method of playing "out" involves taking a structure and moving it (without changing its note relationships) to places other than where we started. If a group of notes starts "inside" the harmony, once we establish it, we can move it around, and our ears will often accept it.

Arrangers use the term "constant structure" to describe creating a voicing, and maintaining the intervallic note relationships of the structure as you follow the melodic line. Figure 7.26 demonstrates constant structure of a melody. Notice how many "wrong" notes are present in the structure once it starts to move with the melody.

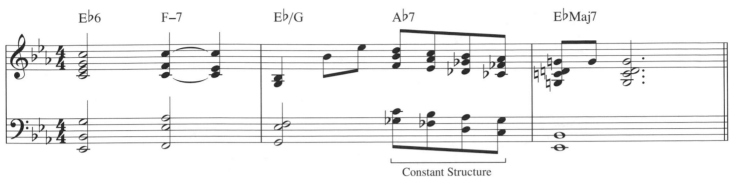

Fig. 7.26. Melodic Line with Constant Structure Voicing

We can use this method in our solos by creating a melodic structure, and moving it without altering its intervallic relationships as shown in the graphic below.

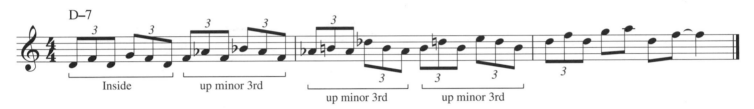

Fig. 7.27. Melodic Line with Constant Structure Voicing

After playing an "inside" phrase over the D–7, I have moved the exact phrase (with identical note relationships intact) "outside" of the typical D–7 chord scales and then resolve back to D Dorian as labeled in figure 7.27.

How far and how often the movement occurs is up to you. You might try a simple half step up, or a tritone away. It usually makes sense to establish what sounds "inside" before moving "outside," and then to return to the "inside." This type of approach is similar to a dominant chord resolving to a tonic. Start with very short and simple phrases at first, and when you find ones you like, write them in your notebook. Label the chord type and the pattern of movement so you can practice them in all keys.

Figures 7.28 and 7.29 are examples demonstrating movement between "inside" and "outside" using constant structure phrases.

Fig. 7.28. Inside and Outside Motifs

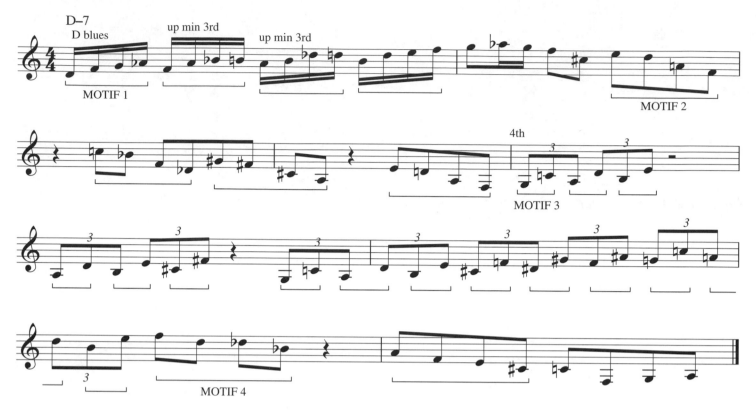

Fig. 7.29. Inside and Outside Motifs 2

Since there is really no definitive process of playing "outside," anything is possible. You could inject non-functional chords or melodic lines into what you are playing, but what makes it work is your personal vision of what you are creating. How well any of these methods work is also going to depend on the musicians around you and their ability to adapt to what you are suggesting with your musical choices. I strongly believe that the study and preparation of specific skills allows us to have those magical moments where art is created.

Modes of the Major Scale

1. DORIAN

C Dorian

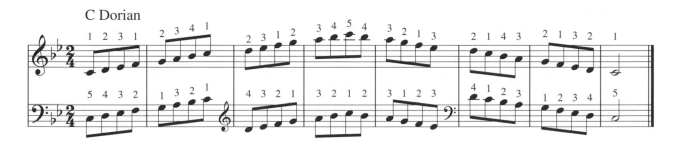

F Dorian

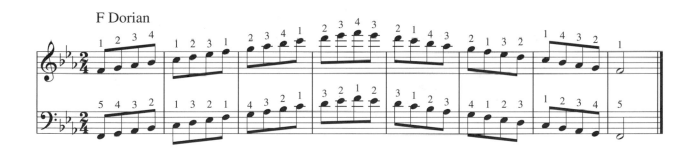

B♭ Dorian

E♭ Dorian

Ab Dorian

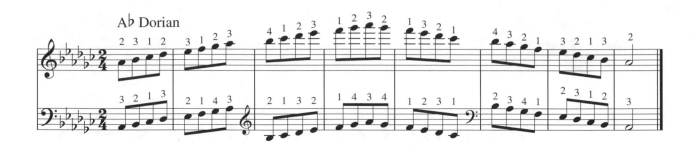

C# Dorian

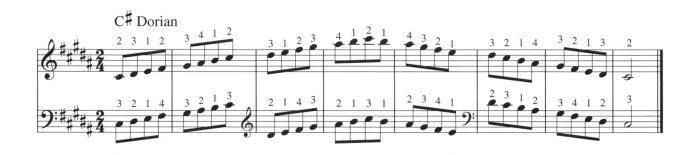

F# Dorian

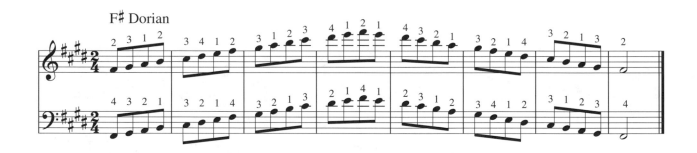

B Dorian

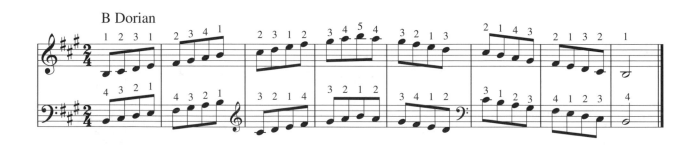

E Dorian

A Dorian

D Dorian

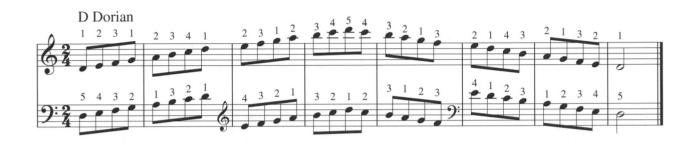

G Dorian

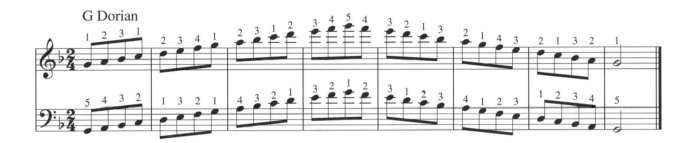

2. PHRYGIAN

C Phrygian

F Phrygian

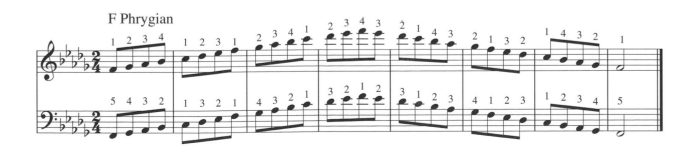

Bb Phrygian

D# Phrygian

G# Phrygian

C# Phrygian

F# Phrygian

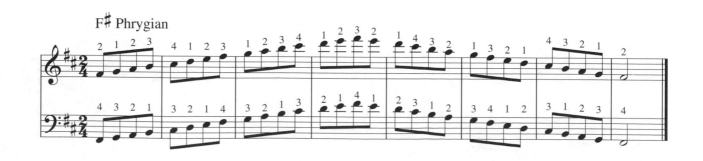

B Phrygian

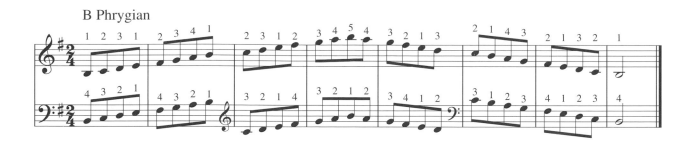

E Phrygian

A Phrygian

D Phrygian

G Phrygian

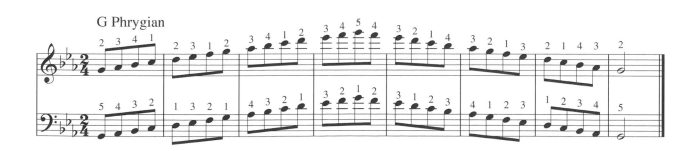

D Lydian

G Lydian

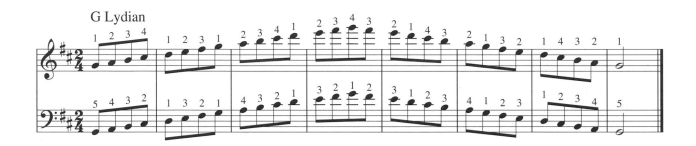

4. MIXOLYDIAN

C Mixolydian

F Mixolydian

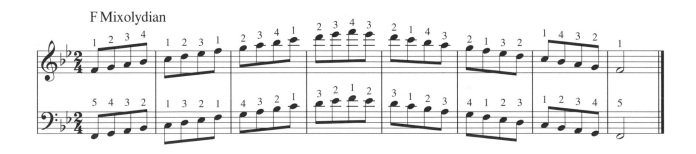

Bb Mixolydian

Eb Mixolydian

Ab Mixolydian

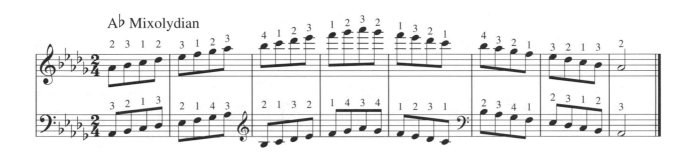

Db Mixolydian

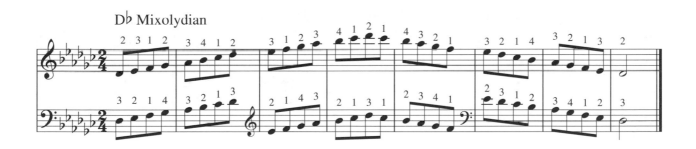

F# Mixolydian

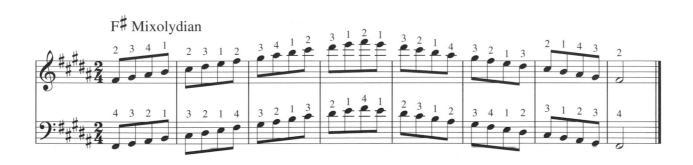

B Mixolydian

E Mixolydian

A Mixolydian

D Mixolydian

G Mixolydian

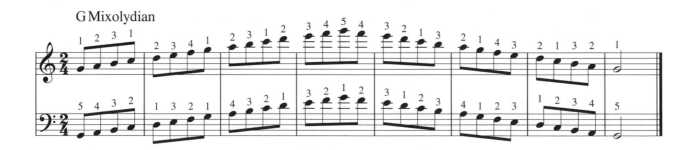

5. AEOLIAN

C Aeolian

F Aeolian

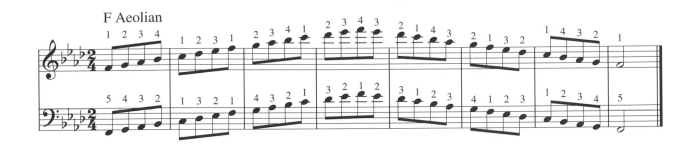

B♭ Aeolian

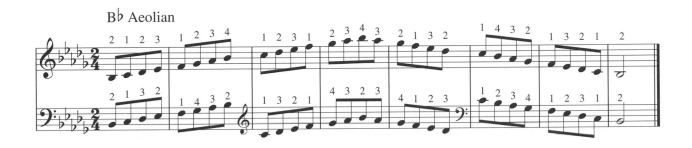

E♭ Aeolian

G♯ Aeolian

C♯ Aeolian

F# Aeolian

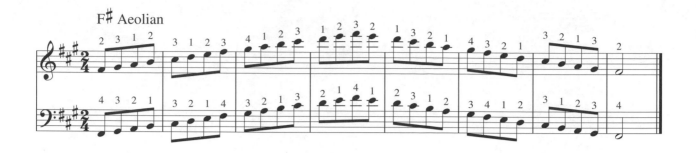

B Aeolian

E Aeolian

A Aeolian

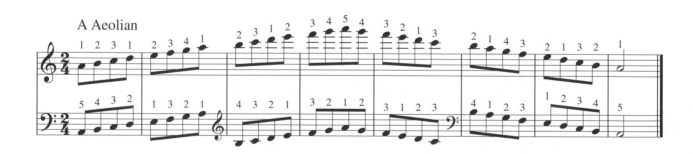

D Aeolian

G Aeolian

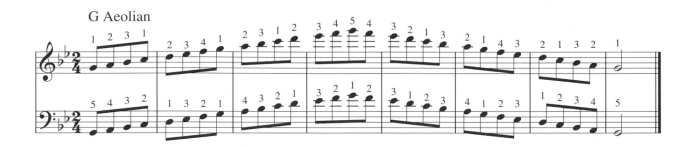

6. LOCRIAN

C Locrian

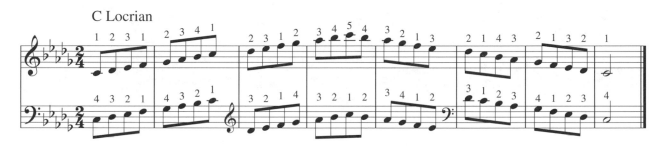

F Locrian

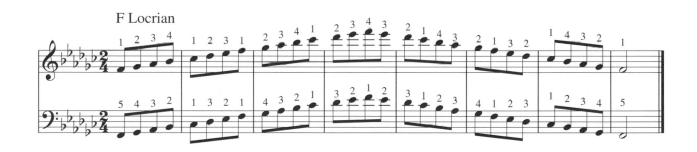

A# Locrian

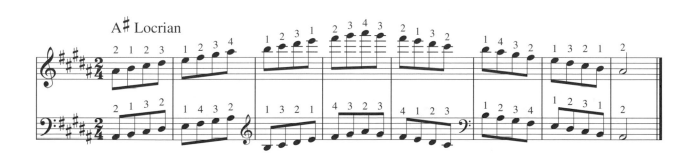

D# Locrian

G# Locrian

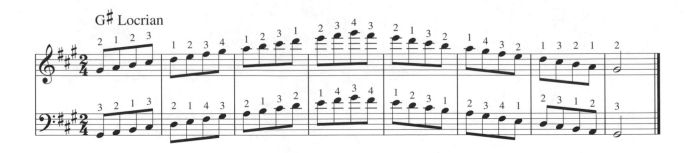

C# Locrian

F# Locrian

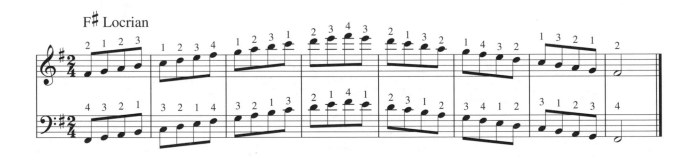

B Locrian

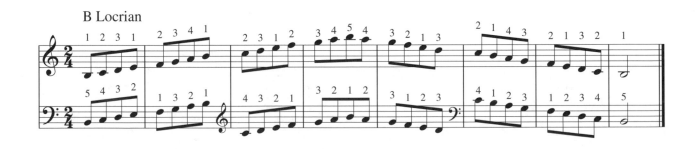

E Locrian

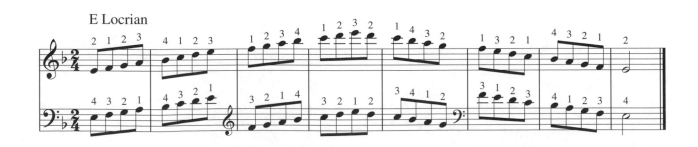

A Locrian

D Locrian

G Locrian

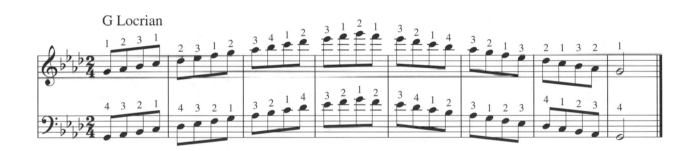

Modes of the Minor Scale

1. LYDIAN ♭7

C Lydian ♭7

F Lydian ♭7

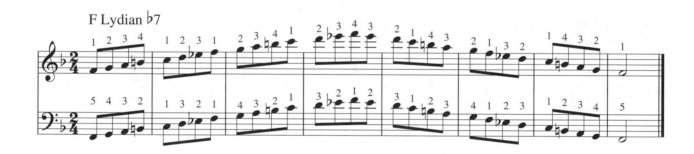

B♭ Lydian ♭7

E♭ Lydian ♭7

Ab Lydian b7

Db Lydian b7

Gb Lydian b7

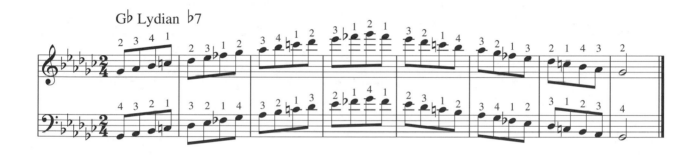

B Lydian b7

E Lydian b7

A Lydian ♭7

D Lydian ♭7

G Lydian ♭7

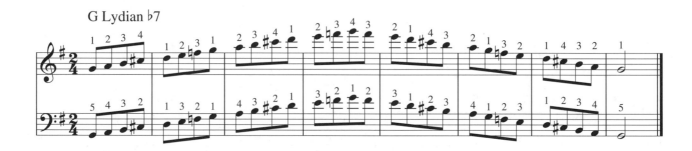

2. LOCRIAN NATURAL 9

C Locrian Natural 9

F Locrian Natural 9

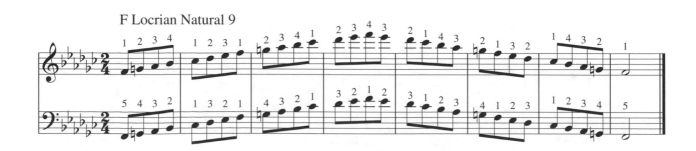

B♭ Locrian Natural 9

D♯ Locrian Natural 9

G♯ Locrian Natural 9

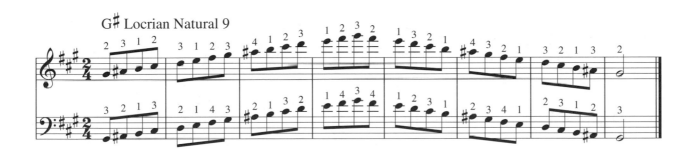

C♯ Locrian Natural 9

F♯ Locrian Natural 9

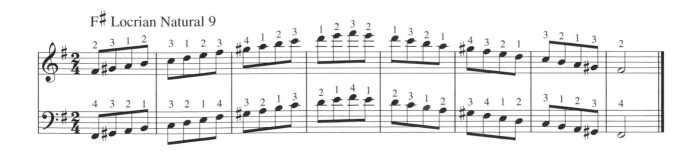

B Locrian Natural 9

E Locrian Natural 9

A Locrian Natural 9

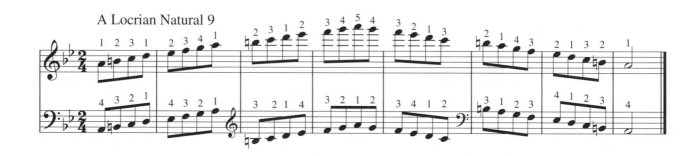

D Locrian Natural 9

G Locrian Natural 9

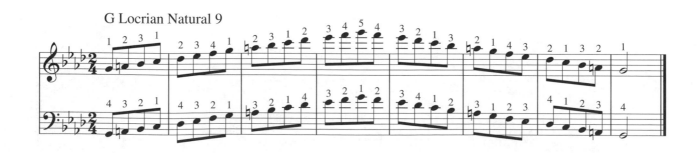

3. ALTERED

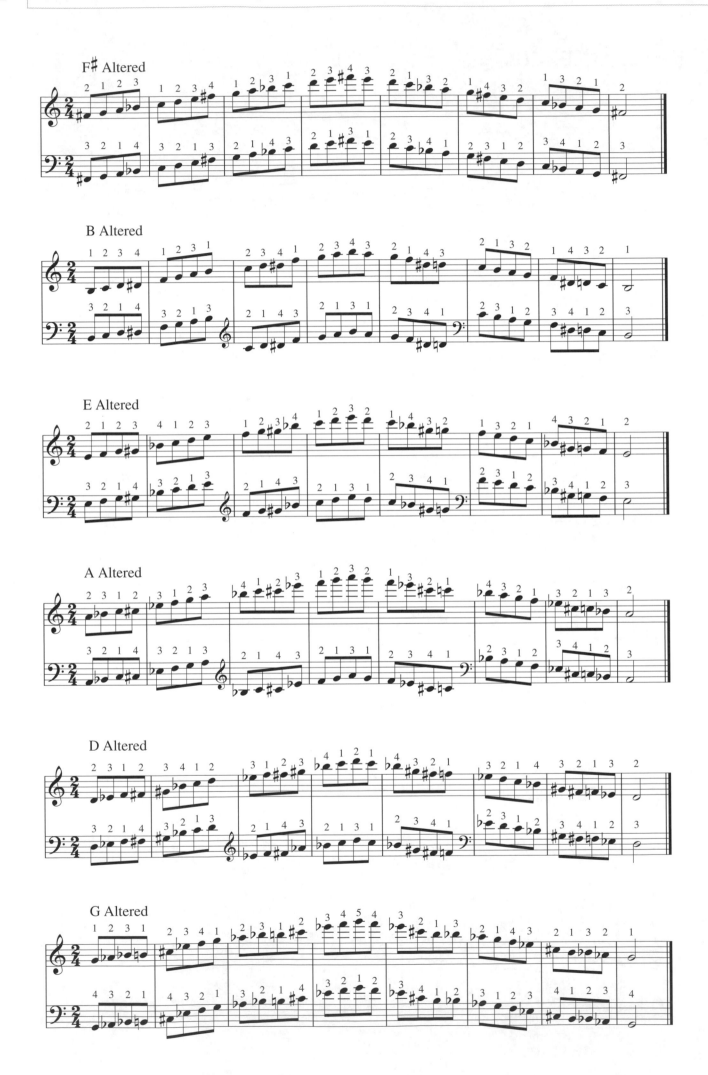

APPENDIX C

Blues Scales

C Blues

F Blues

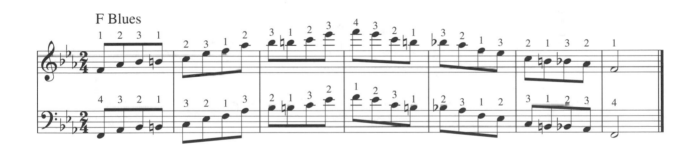

B♭ Blues

E♭ Blues

A♭ Blues

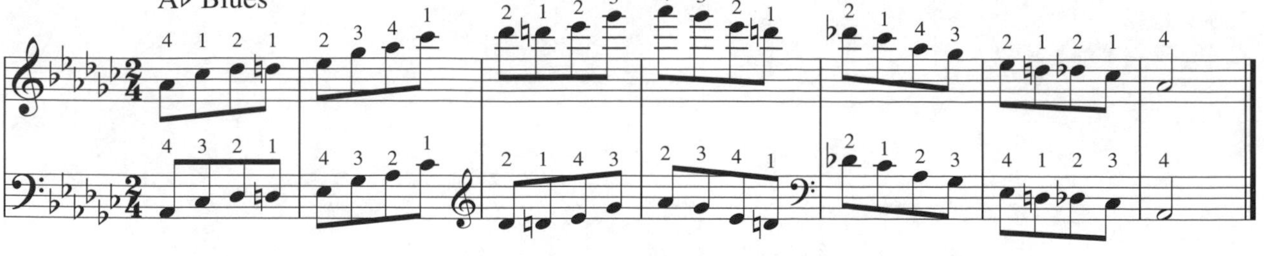

C♯ Blues

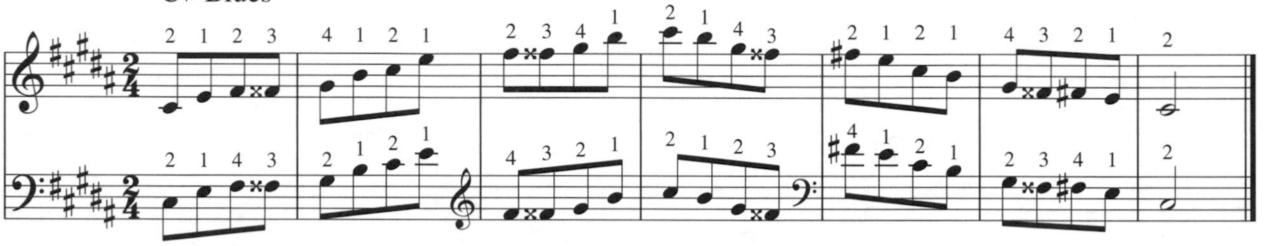

F♯ Blues

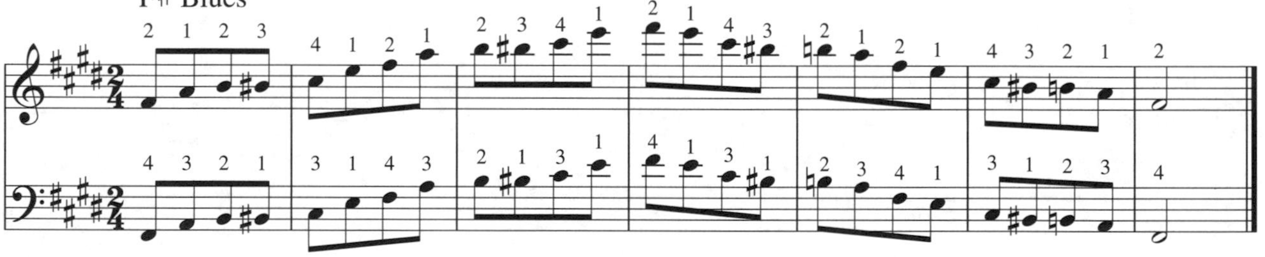

B Blues

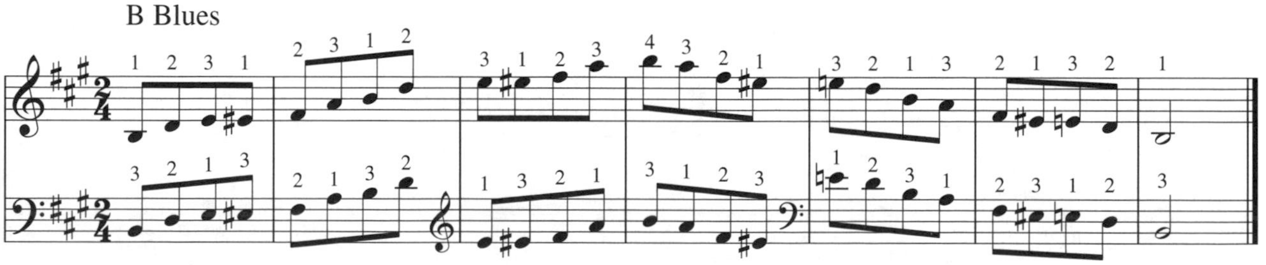

E Blues

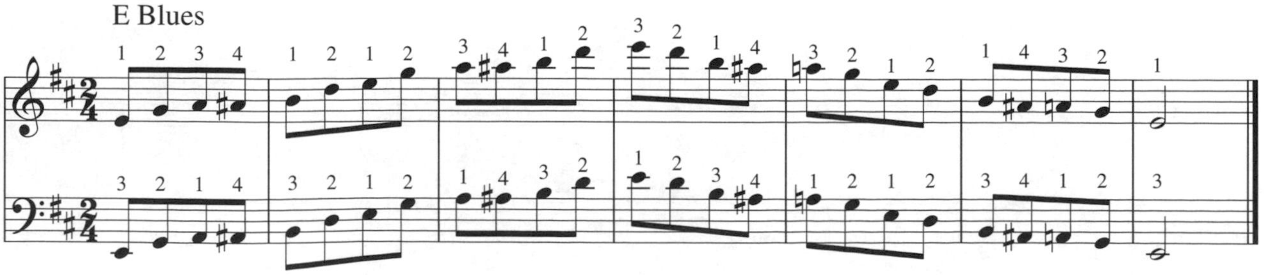

APPENDIX D

Symmetrical Scales

1. WHOLE/HALF DIMINISHED

C Whole/Half Diminished

E♭ Whole/Half Diminished

F♯ Whole/Half Diminished

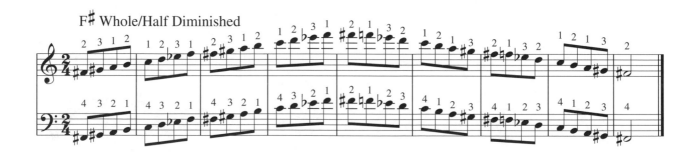

A Whole/Half Diminished

C# Whole/Half Diminished

E Whole/Half Diminished

G Whole/Half Diminished

Bb Whole/Half Diminished

D Whole/Half Diminished

F Whole/Half Diminished

A♭ Whole/Half Diminished

B Whole/Half Diminished

2. HALF/WHOLE DIMINISHED

C Half/Whole Diminished

E♭ Half/Whole Diminished

F# Half/Whole Diminished

A Half/Whole Diminished

C# Half/Whole Diminished

E Half/Whole Diminished

G Half/Whole Diminished

Bb Half/Whole Diminished

D Half/Whole Diminished

F Half/Whole Diminished

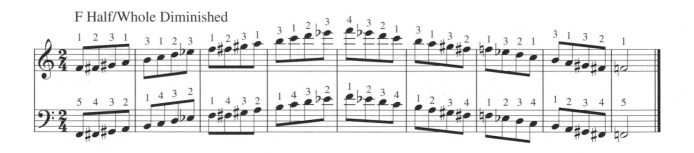

Ab Half/Whole Diminished

B Half/Whole Diminished

3. WHOLE TONE SCALE

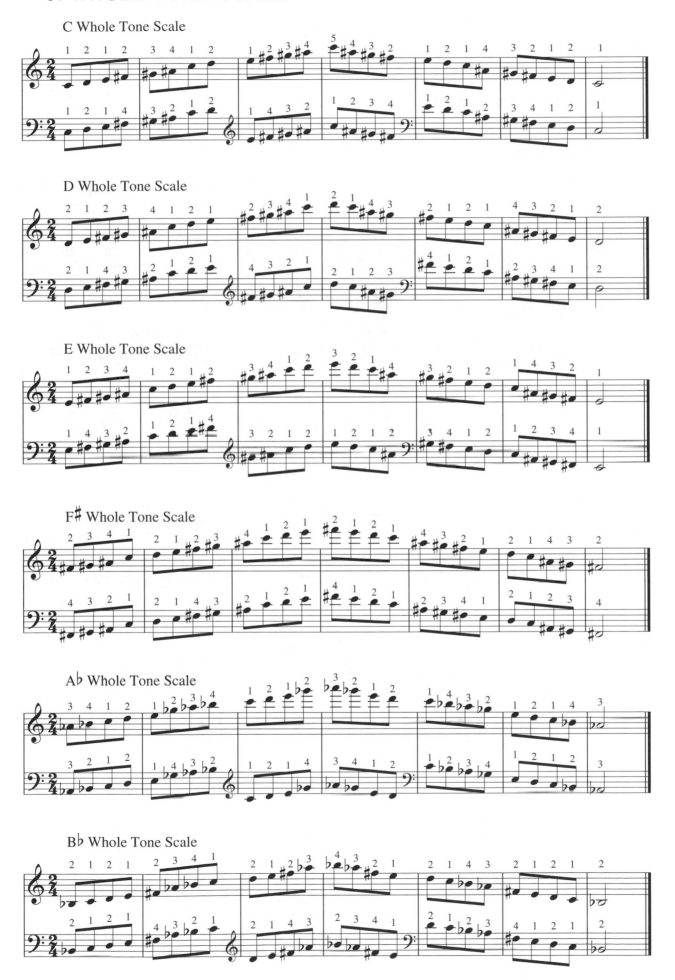

D♭ Whole Tone Scale

E♭ Whole Tone Scale

F Whole Tone Scale

G Whole Tone Scale

A Whole Tone Scale

B Whole Tone Scale

Conclusion

"Chance favors the prepared mind."

—Louis Pasteur

Keep in mind that the goal is for you to play ideas that you already can imagine in your head. When you play your instrument, you want to express your thoughts so that everyone else can hear what you are thinking. The goal of practicing all of these exercises and techniques is to increase your awareness of the language and give you the ability to harness it by developing your playing facility. If you have no connection aurally to what you are playing, then it's not going to sound very good.

Listen carefully to what you are playing, and spend a lot of time listening to other professional performers and transcribing their solos.

About the Author

Ross Ramsay has been teaching music professionally for over twenty-five years. In 2001, he joined the Piano Department at Berklee College of Music where he teaches private piano studies, ensembles, and serves as adjunct professor in the Electronic Production and Design Department, teaching music technology. At Berkleemusic, Berklee's online continuing education division, Ross authored and teaches *Producing Music with Cubase*, co-authored and teaches *Berklee Jazz Piano Method*, and teaches *Berklee Keyboard Method* and *Desktop Music Production for Mac*.

Ross is also an active pianist and composer producing music for local and nationally broadcast television, radio, cable, and video programs. He has been a featured soloist on piano and keyboards with various artists touring throughout the United States and Europe and has worked as a product specialist and clinician for Yamaha Corporation of America. His first book, *Piano Essentials: Scales, Chords, Arpeggios, and Cadences for the Contemporary Pianist*, is available through Berklee Press/Hal Leonard. He received a bachelor of music from Berklee College of Music in 1986. Please visit Rossramsay.com for more information.